Necronomicon

Book Five

D1437741

Noir Publishing
10 Spinney Grove
Hereford
HR1 1AY
email:noirpub@dsl.pipex.com
www.noirpublishing.co.uk

Necronomicon Book Five
Edited by: Andy Black
ISBN 9780953656455
© Andy Black and all contributors 2007, all rights reserved
First published 2007 by:
Noir Publishing
Copyright © Noir Publishing 2007
Necronomicon - a periodical publication
Photographs taken from the Noir Publishing Collection & reproduced in
the spirit of publicity
Cover Photo:
Monster Man By courtesy of Metro Tartan Films
Back Photo:
Resident Evil By courtesy of Columbia Tristar Home Entertainment

Editor's Acknowledgements
Sterling work from many an individual has aided the production of this
volume but special mention to Paul at Tartan, Liz at Lions Gate, Sally at
CBC, Jim Harper, Steve Earles and all my contributors.

British Library Cataloguing in Publication Data:
A catalogue record for this book is available from the British Library

Contents

Some six years have elapsed since the last *Necronomicon* book emerged from the fetid cult film undergrowth, so my ever lengthening publishing schedules have surpassed themselves in the production of this volume.

There have been some interesting genre trends in this hiatus but my own personal favourite has been the unexpectedly triumphant return of one of the horror films staple monsters, the zombie. Not only has the master George Romero returned with **Land of the Dead** and the newly released **Diary of the Dead**, but these shores have also echoed to the zombie march in style if not name with Danny Boyle's captivating **28 Days Later**, as well as the much maligned but generally entertaining **Resident Evil** trilogy (thus far at any rate!).

An equally pervasive theme has been the emergence of the 'torture-porn' films ignited by the **Hostel** series and an equally fragmented world which remains a far cry from the post war, not to mention cold war concerns espoused in Matthew Edwards piece on **The Thing** and Steve Earles **Quatermass and the Pit**/*John Carpenter* entry.

Whether it is the sultry form of Sarah Michelle Gellar in Adrian Horrocks **Buffy the Vampire Slayer** or the sexual motifs and murders in Melanie Dante's opus that floats your boat, there is a diverse mixture of writing here combining the most provoking in European cinema with the most compelling in American cinema.

Without further ado I hope that there will be more than enough within these pages to pique your interest in the films discussed and perhaps inspire some to visit or even revisit specific entries and even bodies of work again.

Until the next time...

Andy Black

November 2007

The First Horror Soap: the innovative genre mix of Buffy the Vampire Slayer.

Adrian Horrocks

The television drama series *Buffy The Vampire Slayer* mixes conventions from soap opera and the horror genre with innovative results. The soap opera's use of continuing characters; interior, dialogue based scenes; focus on female characters; and an interest in relationships, is mixed with the outdoor and violent scenes normally seen in action and horror. Buffy reflects soap's habitual central location around an institution, with many scenes set at school (latterly college), but which has now broadened to include the whole of the town of Sunnydale. The ironically named Sunnydale is situated over a 'Hellmouth', a place which attracts supernatural events of all kinds, allowing Buffy to fight a variety of different monsters, whilst limiting her to a single location. In addition to mixing post *Hill Street* series drama with horror, *Buffy* is a teenage drama, a form which often combines with other marginal genres, although the show is now quickly developing an adult tone.

The horror genre emphasises action, and has been successful in films, as its self-contained stories have the freedom to surprise the audience about which characters will survive. The only continuing characters tend to be monsters, who the films are often named for, and who reappear in sequels. Horror on TV has been mainly confined to anthology shows, which have self-contained stories and present new characters in each episode. Rod Serling's *The Twilight Zone* has been followed by numerous other anthology shows in both US and the UK, including *Night Gallery*, *Tales of The Unexpected*, *Hammer House of Horror*, *Tales From the Crypt* and *Urban Gothic*. Anthology shows allow the horror genre to avoid taking account of the structure of television drama, as they are actually unconnected short films grouped under a shared heading. Like films, they have predetermined endings: the story moves towards its conclusion, and there are clues along the way as to what this will be. Twist endings make this predetermined conclusion even more crucial, as they contain the entire point of the preceding tale. These resolved endings put horror in opposition to TV genres such as soap opera and series drama, which are perpetually in

Buffy the Vampire Slayer

the middle of their stories, always putting off their end, which would mean the end of the show.

Stretching out the middle of the story allows television to present evolving characters whom the audience can get to know and share their lives with. This distinctively televisual pleasure is something the horror anthologies are unable to present, making them less engaging than other TV genres. *The X Files* has continuing central characters, but most of its episodes are stand-alone, with a different monster featuring each week. Although its continuing characters allow the opportunity for character growth, *The X Files* has not effectively managed this, and instead a convoluted science-fiction conspiracy plot has been introduced, making the show unintelligible to casual viewers, and taking it further from recognisable characterisation.

The horror genre habitually presents female characters as victims, without continuing lives. In her book *Men Women and Chainsaws* (1992), Carol J Clover has argued that the last horror movie survivor is often female: the 'Final Girl'.*i* Nevertheless, such female characters are not presented in depth, and only assume importance towards the climax, as their name suggests. Clover has also indicated that the Final Girl is not fully female. As stand-in for the male viewer, she must be chaste, and aggressive. The monster or killer in horror films is usually masculine, and murders a number of helpless female victims before succumbing to the Final Girl. These murders are often sexualised in their presentation, and use phallic imagery such as knives. The Final Girl's victory is also often only temporary, as the monster may return for a sequel, but the Final Girl usually doesn't.

If horror marginalises female characters, soap does the opposite, making the ongoing dramas of female characters its central concern. Male characters are less capable than females, and have peripheral roles, either manipulated by strong females, or simply being destructive monsters. Soap includes many interior scenes, in which characters discuss their problems. They are usually based around a single location, often an institution. Problems are worked out through talk, rather than action. The continuing stories of soap allow characters to remember past events, with the result, as Ellis puts it, that: "...there is time for sub-plots to develop, for incidental characters to take on a life of their own, and for the dramatic intensity of the clash of single characters to give way to the dramatic complexities of ensemble work."*ii*

Teenage culture is a relatively new phenomena, and has also been seen as a marginal one, existing at the peripheries. As such, James Hay sees teenage culture as having an outsider's affinity for other marginal cultural forms, such as horror and melodrama, and often mixes with these genres as a result.*iii* Teenage horror films first began in the late 1950's, with such low budget fare as **I Was a Teenage Werewolf** (Fowler, 1957) and **Teenagers from Outer Space** (Graeff, 1959), in which the alien nature of the teenager is perceived as a natural fit with the otherworldly science fiction and horror elements. By contrast, what Hay calls 'clean teenpics' use elements of melodrama, or 'women's pictures', and have female leads. While the teenpic mixed with both horror and melodrama in separate films, horror and women's films were still seen as mutually exclusive, and did not mix.

The series drama has changed substantially during the past ten years. This change is largely attributable to the innovative series *Hill Street Blues iv*, which introduced elements of soap opera to prime-time drama. Before *Hill Street*, action-oriented series drama stood in sharp opposition to daytime soap (and to so-called 'evening soaps' such as *Dallas* and *Dynasty*). Series drama was male-orientated, and presented self-assured male characters in action scenarios: *Magnum PI, Miami Vice*. Like the horror anthologies, stories were confined to a single episode, and characters did not remember past events. Unlike horror, the same cast featured each week, but they embarked on a completely new (although often very similar) adventure. As Rosen put it: "With only one hour a week and a much larger male audience, they rely far more on...fast paced action than on the endless analysis of personal conflicts."v *Hill Street Blues* created a combination of the two genres. It added more female characters, and gave male characters emotional lives, and inner struggles, no matter how tough they were. There were also more dialogue scenes. This multi-stranded, soap-style narrative went on to influence a generation of shows such as *LA Law*, *E.R.* and *Ally McBeal*, to the extent that series drama is now a kind of "discontinuous soap."vi The series drama differs from soap in that it has a limited number of episodes, but can return for a further series. The horror genre, with its reliance on resolved endings, did not respond to these changes, and continued to produce anthology shows, or action-orientated series, making it seem apart from the rest of the schedules, and dated.

The television series *Buffy The Vampire Slayer* has successfully adapted the horror genre to the demands of post-*Hill Street* series drama. Mixing horror with soap elements has proved to be an innovative and successful combination, with each adding depth to the other. However, the mix was not immediately apparent. Buffy was inspired by the horror-comedy film **Buffy the Vampire Slayer** (Kuzui 1992), written by the creator of the television series, Joss Whedon. The film centred on a single conflict between Buffy and an all-powerful vampire Master. Following in the wake of horror-comedies such as **Fright Night** (Holland 1985), the film relied for its appeal on the humorous juxtaposition of the girlish name Buffy with her unlikely occupation. The TV *Buffy* debuted in 1995, and initially attempted to follow the same formula as the film, with the introduction of a vampire Master for Buffy to battle, and setting up the expectation of a resolved ending for the season finale. Like *The X Files*, season one of *Buffy* had many stand-alone stories, and there was little memory of past events, or internal character struggle. Although supporting characters were introduced, they were shallow, and existed only in their relationship to Buffy. Best friend Willow was less attractive than Buffy, while pretty Cordelia was bitchy, to make Buffy seem sweeter. Xander's main trait was his unsatisfied lust for Buffy, Giles was a stuffy surrogate

father. Using the dated model of action-orientated series drama, and moving towards a resolved series ending, the first season of *Buffy* had only its female characters to distinguish it from the tired 1980's action dramas, or stand-alone horror anthologies. Nevertheless, the use of Buffy's name in the show's title showed her to be more important than any individual monster, and allowed the potential for a radical soap-horror mix.

During the second season of the show, *Buffy* began to take account of the greater soap elements of post-*Hill Street* series drama. The introduction of vampires Spike and Drusilla created two romantic triangles between them, Buffy and Angel. From 'What's My Line?' (season two, 2ABB09) onwards, the continuing story-line of Buffy's romance with Angel assumed greater importance, continuing in combination with stand-alone stories. While the film version of *Buffy* ridiculed its characters, and the first season of the show foregrounded action, from the second season onwards *Buffy* has treated its characters' feelings and problems with the seriousness of soap, while still including horror scenes. *Buffy* now mixes soap opera and horror from a teenage perspective. This shift hasn't pushed the show outside the boundaries of teenage drama, as according to Ellis, soaps have great appeal to teenagers, as they provide "modern society's 'apprentice adults' with a wide range of narrativised dilemmas."*vii*

Buffy the Vampire Slayer

In *Buffy*, the horror and soap genres combine to reflect on each other. The show's soap elements, typified by interior scenes, where mainly female characters explore their feelings through talk, mix with horror tropes such as male characters and outdoor action scenes. The latter are not included for simple scares, as in the horror anthologies. Instead, the horror imagery in Buffy externalises and illuminates the emotions contained in the show's soap elements. Using the conventions of the horror genre to present characters' internal feelings in an allegorical manner refreshes what would otherwise be over-familiar scenarios of love, romantic betrayal and soured friendship. Character problems are rendered more dramatic, are universalised, and are of greater importance through the use of horror conventions: they become literally matters of life and death. Sexual encounters can be presented allegorically as well as literally, such as Buffy's exchange of blood with Angel. An example of *Buffy*'s mixture of interior soap, and outdoor horror can be seen in 'Dead Man's Party' (season three, 3ABB02). Interior scenes of a highly emotional argument between Buffy and her mother and Willow, are inter-cut with outdoor scenes of Giles fighting marauding zombies. As the argument reaches its peak, the zombies burst into the house, providing a release for the tensions in the talk, while bringing characters and genres together.

Faith is a familiar soap character, who uses sarcastic talk to undermine the protagonists, and she has seduced both Xander and Riley, simply to hurt Buffy and Willow. Buffy and Faith are Slayers, and have super-powers. Willow and Tara are witches, adept with spells. Anya is a demon who has willingly given up her powers, to become Xander's girlfriend. These supernatural horror elements provide a rationale for the female characters being at the centre of the drama, and empower them to remain there effectively. Where a soap opera would present Buffy and Faith arguing, in Buffy they clash both verbally and physically, heightening the stakes of the encounter. Soaps often bring in new characters, but this can feel awkward. The supernatural elements in *Buffy* allowed the addition of Dawn to be a fascinating puzzle, while at the same time retrospectively adding a younger character to compensate for the rest of the cast growing older. The introduction of Dawn has also allowed an allegorical study of sibling rivalry, with Buffy's feelings that her little sister was an intruder ringing true on both psychological and horror story levels. Dawn's resulting alienation has also allowed the show to deal with teenage self-loathing, through the lens of the horror genre.

Angel's vampiric nature gives epic status to his role as the bad boy Buffy finds irresistible. As a vampire, Angel's unsuitability for Buffy is made obvious, and tragically insurmountable. The teenage pain of an intense, doomed relationship is given greater emotional weight through the use of horror devices. Under a gypsy curse, Angel becomes the evil Angelus if he experiences pure happiness, justifying his habitual sullen moodiness. His night with Buffy activates the curse, proving he truly loves her. This provides an allegorical, and resonant rationale for Angel dumping Buffy after he sleeps with her (which are the actions of a villainous soap opera character), whilst also excusing him. Angel goes on to kill Jenny Calendar, Giles' gypsy girlfriend. Having a vampire kill a woman is a standard horror device, but the murder has ongoing consequences for the characters' relationships, as Giles turns against Angel, whilst Buffy still loves him, giving a standard clash between daughter and father figure over an unsuitable boyfriend much greater power than it would otherwise have.

In line with soap opera conventions, male characters such as Giles, Xander and Spike have smaller roles than their female counterparts, and exist to offer support, or request help from them. Xander is often seen as a figure of fun, with jokes constructed specifically around his masculinity. As in horror, monsters are often masculine, such as Adam. However, the presence of strong female characters shifts the balance, and such monsters cannot simply kill unchallenged, as they can in horror. The Geek trio (which includes the previously featured characters of Jonathan and Warren) are simply buffoons, ridiculed for their love of sci-fi, even though they have the ability to build robots, and distort time. Buffy's two boyfriends fare little better. Buffy sends Angel to hell, while Riley is her inferior in every way, a solider content to follow orders without question. Riley belongs to the all-male military group The Initiative, dullards ignorant of the evil motives of their matriarchal leader Professor Walsh. 'The Yoko Factor' (season four, 4ABB20) has the tall, muscular Angel and Riley face off, about to fight over the diminutive Buffy standing between them. Her response: "I will personally put you both in the hospital", avoids the clichéd scenes of soap, while underscoring that this heroine has the physical as well as the emotional strength to solve such conflicts. Unlike the 'Final Girl', Buffy is strong but also fully feminine, having romantic attachments, and emotional

crises, which are explored over many episodes.

Since its adoption of soap elements, *Buffy*'s supporting characters have developed strengths and relationships of their own, such as Willow's witchcraft, and Xander and Cordelia's brief tryst. Secondary characters have now been introduced, whose strongest relationship is to the supporting characters, with little link of their own to Buffy. Oz and Tara are primarily linked to Willow, Anya's main relationship is with Xander. These characters are necessary, to fill the time available once continuing plots are used. Without them, Buffy could not survive, any more than they could without her. The symbiotic nature of Buffy's relationship to these characters has been highlighted in several episodes, notably 'Primeval' (season four, 4ABB21), in which they link telepathically with Buffy, who is only then able to battle Adam, strengthened by her friends' support. The following episode, 'Restless', (season four, 4ABB22), again requires teamwork, and Buffy rejects the message of The First Slayer, who tells her that she should be alone. Nevertheless, Buffy's presence remains most crucial.

In 'Anne' (season three, 3ABB01) Buffy leaves Sunnydale, and her friends try to carry on battling demons without her, with limited success. They repeatedly speak of Buffy, and do not feel complete without her, acknowledging that the show cannot continue without its main character. For her part, Buffy feels incomplete on her own, and returns. After Buffy's death, 'Bargaining' (season six, 6ABB01/02) Willow is a much stronger character, but is still unable to continue without the show's main character, whom she raises from the dead. In 'The Wish' (season three 3ABB09), Cordelia rebels against her supporting role by changing time so that Buffy never comes to Sunnydale. As a result, vampires overrun the town, and Willow and Xander become a ruthless vampire couple, who kill Cordelia. Although it is unsurprising that Cordelia and the others do not fare well without Buffy, the episode also shows the relationship to be mutual, with the climatic introduction of an alternate Buffy. New to the town, and without having had the opportunity to befriend the now undead Willow and Xander, this Buffy is an angry loner, and is swiftly killed by the vampire Master.

Buffy's continuing story-lines last for the length of a season, before being resolved in the final episode. A new story-line is premiered in the first episode of the subsequent season. This lets characters remember past events, and learn and change, an element lacking in horror, even in sequels. Each season sees Buffy tackling a new major threat, ('The Big Bad') which becomes increasingly dangerous, until it is resolved in the final episode. Characters remember these past threats, and refer to them. The audience is also aware of them, and uses knowledge of past events to try and read ahead of the text, something which is one of TV's pleasures. viii The writers of the show are aware of the audience's anticipation of a new Big Bad at the beginning of each new season, and have responded by simultaneously confounding and satisfying this anticipation by setting up a particular character for this role; such as Professor Walsh in season four; only to have them superseded, or summarily killed, by the real threat; in this case Adam. The introduction of Dawn at the start of season five suggested that she would be the major villain, before revealing Glory as the true threat. Such sophisticated play with viewer expectations marks *Buffy* out as distinctive. Dawn's introduction also played with viewers' memories of past events on the show. Her sudden appearance challenged the link established by the shared memories of viewers and characters, as the characters remembered Dawn as having always been present, while viewers knew she was a new arrival.

Like all series drama, *Buffy* is a narrative which is evolving. The cast have become older, and the series has reflected this, moving them from High School to college. The tone of the stories has also become more adult in both its soap and horror elements, as the characters' view of the world moves from adolescent to adult. Because the horror elements make *Buffy*'s problems of global importance, it is more credible that her friends would be inclined to stay with her as they grow up, rather than naturally scattering. Initially, Buffy lived with her mother at home, and attended school. She then moved to a nearby Sunnydale college dorm, whilst attending university, before moving back home after her mother's death, and the home now developing into a shared house with her friends. The soap elements mean that *Buffy* must reflect the typical changes in circumstances experienced as teenagers grow up, but with the difference that for her they all occur in a single location. *Buffy*'s increasingly adult tone has caused scheduling problems, as its genre mix is now making it difficult to fit the show into a schedule built around easily defined shows. Initially an earlier slot was as natural for *Buffy* as it was for such fare as *Star Trek* and *Hollyoaks*, because both the horror and soap elements were controlled to some extent by the teenage ones, (although the BBC has habitually censored the show's violence.) Now that the characters are growing up, the challenges that they face are not only more violent, but also reflect on their characters in allegories which are more mature. Willow's magic addiction is a clear drug allegory. Buffy's highly-charged and explicit affair with Spike is far more adult in its presentation than her previous relationships.

The maturing of *Buffy*'s genre mix has also led the show to become increasingly ambitious, and several episodes have added other genres to the usual mix of horror and soap. In 'Superstar'(season four, 4ABB17), the minor character of Jonathan takes centre stage, becoming the lead. The opening titles are altered, presenting the show as an action adventure in the genre of *Magnum PI* or *The A Team*. The episode satirised the more masculine genre, while letting *Buffy* play with the tropes it had once used in earnest. 'Restless' (season four, 4ABB22), is set in the characters' dreams, and includes images reminiscent of writer/director David Lynch, a genre to himself. In 'The Body' (season five, 5ABB16), Buffy's mother dies. The episode dispenses with both horror and soap, to adopt an adult, but still non-realist tone. 'The Body' includes Buffy's subjective fantasies of her mother's resurrection, mixed with an objective look at her death. The vast difference in the presentation of the death of Buffy's mother from all previous deaths on the show, suggests that she may be the only character to have truly died, the others being symbolic deaths, indicating Buffy's triumphs over the struggles of her life. The appearance of a vampire towards the end of the episode signals that such problems will continue. 'Once More With Feeling' (season six, 6ABB07), is a musical episode, with characters bursting into a succession of songs, whose staging and tunes consciously evokes the conventions of the film musical. Both horror and soap elements remain readily apparent: a demon is responsible, the songs can have fatal consequences, and although the lyrics begin jolly, they soon start to reveal secrets that the characters would rather have left unspoken.

Buffy the Vampire Slayer succeeds as soap, and the heightened problems faced by the characters are much more interesting than those in more realist, 'kitchen-sink' dramas. The horror elements sometimes seem subservient to the characters, but this is perhaps inevitable, given the shallow characterisation in much of the genre's output. The use of horror's rules and ideas shows a wide knowledge of the genre, and Buffy has achieved something genuinely innovative: thrilling horror, with involving and evolving characters. The recent episodes which include other genres indicate that the show may still have its best moments to come. Such ambitious episodes see *Buffy* striving towards non-genre specific fantasy, perhaps akin to Patrick McGoohan's *The Prisoner*, but mixing this with an emotional depth of a sort previously only seen on genre television in David Lynch's *Twin Peaks*.

i Carol J. Clover, *Men Women and Chainsaws: Gender in the Modern Horror Film* (London: BFI Publishing, 1992) p.212

ii John Ellis, *Seeing Things: Television in the Age of Uncertainty,* (London: I.B. Tauris, 2000), p.123

iii James Hay, '"You're tearing me apart!": the primal scene of teen films', *Cultural Studies 4(3)*, 1990

iv Todd Gitlin, *Inside Prime Time* (London: Routledge, 1994) p.11

v Ruth Rosen, 'Soap Operas: Search for Yesterday' in *Watching Television*, Todd Gitlin (ed.), (New York: Pantheon Books, 1986) p.51

vi Ellis, ibid.

vii Ellis, ibid.

viii Glaessner, p.118

SCARIER THAN MONSTERS!

Sexual Murder in Art and Film -

From Weimar to the United States

Melanie Dante

"Lustmord" means sexual murder. " Lust" being sexual. "Mord" meaning murder. At the beginning of the 20th century there were a handful of serial killers that had been caught in the Weimar Republic for heinous multiple murders. Fritz Haarman, for example influenced Fritz Lang, Alfred Doblin and everyday citizens like Alfred Hrdlicka who proposed to have a statue of the notorious sexual serial killer placed in a town square to "provoke thought on enigmas of the nation." Truly, Weimar left a legacy. While people do not seem to reflect on the reality of the serial killers influence behind the art, the art is still glorified.

"Because they are so familiar, so evident, we are culturally blind to the ubiquity of representations of feminine death." (Maria Tatar)

First, let's introduce the most famous of murderers caught, and then introduce the artists. The artists did not sublimate the killers; they took their fascination with murder in general to canvas, page, and screen with much public enthusiasm.

"Oh country of opposites and extremes!" writes the narrator of Yvan Goll's *Sodom Berlin* as he reflects on Germany, a place that brought forth the poet Freidrich Holderlin, and the psychopath Fritz Haarman.

Holderlin opened his own veins one day to "water a rose tree". Haarman drank the blood of blond boy loves. Haarman was executed in 1925 for committing nearly thirty murders in Hanover. His victims all died by a severe bite to the throat while they were sleeping. Haarman had disposed of their bodies by chopping them, and throwing them into the Leine River. Wilhelm Grossmann was known as the "Bluebeard of the Silesian Railway", and was charged in 1921 with the murder and cannibalism of fourteen women. Denke was referred to as " The Mass

M

Murderer of Munsterburg". During his brief stay in jail, where he committed suicide by hanging himself, he was known as "Vater Denke". Once a year, for thirty years, he committed murder in his home, and brought buckets of blood out to his courtyard where he would water the plants. He was caught after trying to kill a beggar that came to his door. The peasant contacted the police. When they arrived the authorities found human bones, pickled body parts, fingers, human teeth, and human skin suspenders. Lastly, there was Peter Kurten. The name may ring a bell if you saw the film **Copycat** (1995). It is believed that Kurten influenced the character of Grenouille in Peter Suskind's 1985 novel *Parfum (Das Parfum: Die Geschichte eines Morders)* which was a complete success on both sides of the Atlantic. Kurten, a married man and professional who secretly would go out with cosmetics on and viciously murder vagrant women and children. He murdered thirty-five in all with the youngest being thirteen years old. He became known as "das Ratsel Mensch", or in English: "That Enigma Man." Newspapers such as *Berliner Tageblatt* and *Frankfurter Zeitung* ran frequent articles on the killers. The public's fear, ignited with Haarman, had almost been put to rest when the murders of Kurten began to be reported.

What, though, does any of this have to do with fine art? The images of murder, as displayed through the works of Otto Dix, George Grosz, Alfred Doblin and Fritz Lang became synonymous with the modernist movement of the Weimar Republic.

Silence of the Lambs (1991), **Hannibal** (2001), and **Red Dragon** (2002) were all blockbuster films here in modern day America. Based on the novel by Thomas Harris, *Red Dragon* became the film **Manhunter** (1986), directed by Michael Mann. Manhunter was remade into **Silence of the Lambs**, and became a hit series. We are not shocked by that. We accept in our own culture these heinous crimes as art because these films, along with, say, **Kiss the Girls** (1997) and **Along Came a Spider** (2001) do not just glorify murder, the theme is the race to catch the killer. We can fancy our fetish for murder, as long as in the end good wins over evil. Also in that category are **8MM** (1999) directed by Joel Schumacher, and even the somewhat surreal, **In Dreams** (1999), directed by Neil Jordan (**Interview with the Vampire**). They are all a form of what is now called "Realist Horror", a category many feel was begun in America by Sir Alfred Hitchcock with his mastery for depicting the "criminal sexual psychopath" from **Psycho** (1960) to **Frenzy** (1972). Alfred Hitchcock, as a child, was inspired by film maker Fritz Lang. Most well known for his 1927 release of **Metropolis**, Fritz Lang began his cinema career in Weimar. His 1931 film **M** is a seductive and sinister tale of a pedophiliac and murderer. We can assume the position of being shocked by the debauch of Weimar, but if we look at our culture it seems that we, too, are fascinated by those that are willing to represent and explore the wicked ways of those who are criminally and morally "insane". It seems to be a vicarious thrill. As Brian DePalma has been quoted as saying, "I don't particularly want to chop up women, but it seems to work".

Now, back to Weimar where the term "Erregung" stems. "Erregung" is most frequently recruited to describe "an anxious population", it implies a highly emotional state of mass anxiety, but can also denote sexual arousal. The perfect state to aspire to create for a large film audience! Or, originally, audience for art.

"The feminine body has come to be affiliated with the 'polluting world of biology, with the time bound individual, with corrupting flesh, with putrescence of the corpse, with a bad death." In Otto Weininger's turn of the century German study entitled *Sex & Character*, the chief differences between the sexes (is) "greater absorption of the female in the sphere of sexual activities". Women, according to Weininger, are in fact fixated on the body, wholly devoted to sexual matters, to "the spheres of begetting and reproducing"; where as men are free to pursue the matters of the spirit - science, art, religion, philosophy". There is an ideological pressure to view women as fettered to the carnal and to see men as spiritual beings engaged in a noble struggle to free themselves of biologic needs.

Otto Dix. A World War One veteran and painter, Dix became known for his post war artistic productions of post war artistic productions, mutilated female corpses, grotesque urban streetscapes and serene neo classical portraiture. He was "single mindedly devoted to working through primal fears aroused in combat situations, both military and sexual". One of his most famous paintings from 1922 is entitled *Lustmord*, a repeating theme of the time. His work evolved from mutilated women/prostitutes into savage medical landscapes as seen in the 1943 painting entitled *Portrait of the Surgeon, Professor Dr. R. Andler, Singen, in the Operating Room*. The doctor, who is so noble and regal in his countenance, is not even looking at the open belly on which he is operating.

George Grosz: Painter. Distinguished art historian Kenneth Clark says of Grosz' feminine representations, " (All of the) bodies marked by tough surfaces, undisciplined excesses and crude irregularities". He also painted the ruling class and working class in their daily life (though it is noted even by his son that his depictions show them as ugly and vulgar as possible), Grosz became part of the eternal clique of Weimar's sexual murder culture. Like Dix, he has a painting entitled *Lustmord*, created in 1912/13. Grosz became known for his depictions of women/prostitutes being murdered, and for his depictions of men in political bondage. Another depiction of classic modernist Weimar style entitled *Murder on Acker Street* , painted in 1916. In the forefront a woman is dead on her bed, viciously bludgeoned with a meat hacker. In the background a fat man with the face of a shamed and confused child, washes his hands of her blood. Different from the style of his feminine murder art, *For the Fatherland - To the Slaughterhouse*, painted in 1924, shows in firm and bold charcoal, men being forced off to war. A miniature Hitler sits in the lap of a general like a little doll as blindfolded men are forced to the fight.

Grosz was described as being resistant to "representational practices that construct idealized images of female plentitude or perfection (that and his political parody of masculine roles) seem entirely consonant with his Dadaist irreverence towards artistic ideologies".

Alfred Doblin: Author of the well known *Berlin Alexanderplatz: the Story of Franz Biberkopf*, and numerous popular short stories. As opposed to focusing on his famous novel, a short story of his entitled, *The Murder of Buttercup* caught my attention. Maybe because I thought of Vater Denke watering his rose tree with the blood streaming from his own veins; a surreal, morbid, yet fascinating act! I find the image more vampiric than a man in a cape becoming a bat. There is something almost

Silence of the Lambs

Henry - Portrait of a Serial Killer

seductive about it.

The Murder of Buttercup was published in 1910, prior to the war. It is, superficially, not the about the murder of a person, but an innocent flower. The protagonist in the tale, Mr. Michael Fisher, is a dull man with a dull life. One day while out walking with his cane he vents his frustration of being stuck in the rut of a gentleman on a flower he passes during his walk. He takes his walking stick and beheads the flower. As "white blood and yellow foam" flow from the stem of the now beheaded flower, it turns into a cadaver that must be removed from sight. Papers announced that a grown buttercup had been murdered on the path from Immental to St. Otilllie between seven and nine in the evening. "Neither a hardened criminal, nor a crazed psychotic, Mr. Fischer is a "quintessential German businessman, punctilious in his outer habits, but benighted about his inner life. Like Franz Biberkopf (protagonist in *Berlin Alexanderplatz*) he never reflects on the degree to which his violence is motivated by a profound need to punish women, to strike out at "nature", and to reveal secretly at the sight of its vulnerability his destructive force".

The connection between modernist art and extreme sexual violence is not easy to explain or understand, but it is a reality of popular pieces of the 1920s. Charles Bernheimer explains that the theme of prostitution

"simultaneously activates fears of decomposition and decay and stimulates the creation of new artistic strategies, which display that very disintegration and proclaim their modernity". Painting and literature paved the path for cinema, which brings us now Fritz Lang and his film of pedophilia and murder, **M**.

"Because of the loathsome nature of the crime **M** dealt with, there was a problem of how to represent such a crime so that it would not sicken the audience, yet would have full emotional impact. That is why I only

Nekromantik 2

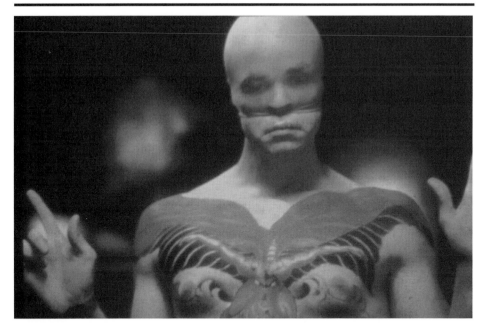

Manhunter

gave hints - the rolling ball, the balloon that caught in the wires, after being released from a little hand. Thus I make the audience an integral part in the creation of this special scene by forcing each individual member of the audience to create the gruesome details of the murder according to his personal imagination." (Fritz Lang)

It is known that Fritz Lang heavily influenced Alfred Hitchcock, but after reading about **M**, it seems he also was a pioneer influence for such ground breaking moments in cinema such as J. Lee Thomson's, **Cape Fear** (1962), released in England with much observation and involvement of the English censor board, and also Stanley Kubrick's, **Lolita** (1962).

Cape Fear is the controversial story of a small town attorney and the ex.convict he sent to jail. Once released the convict returns to haunt the life of the attorney. The ominous threat he ensues by watching the lawyer's young child in a manner that evades the due process of the law. The film was designed to have audiences imagine the worst by not showing or verbalising direct assault, but by alluding to the fact that the young child was to be the target of the ex convicts revenge.

Lolita portrays the love obsession that a middle aged man holds for a twelve year old girl. In Weimar, the love obsession in Lolita also had a specific name; similar to "Lustmord" (sexual murder) , "Liebstod" (love-death) is defined as "the assertion of transcendent desire and the spiritualisation of egos", or by love that is a death, in actuality, of the soul or spirit.

At the time **M** was being contemplated, the newspapers were running continuous articles on the murderers Haarman, Grossmann, Kurten and Denke, forcing to the attention of Fritz Lang the question as to what led these people to commit such acts, and the same question is probably what appealed to audiences when they paid to see the film. Though it added to the thought put into the film, the film was actually inspired by a conversation Lang and his wife Thea Von Harbou had one evening. They were discussing what the most horrible crime to do could be in order to make the plot thick for an interesting film. Ideas were passed back and forth, and they mutually decided on anonymous poisoned letters. They began to collaborate on a film with that theme when Lang thought of the murder of a child, and decided that was the most horrible crime possible. The thought of "a man forced by some urge, by some perverted urge... a sick man ... to kill!" So began the tale of a child murderer whose identity is revealed from the beginning of the film, whose deeds are known by the audience. What is not known is what will happen to the children he meets, to him if / when he is caught, to the families if / when they find out what

Nekromantik 2

Manhunter

has happened to their lost children - the origin, maybe, of films such as **Silence of the Lambs** or **8MM**.

"Although Lang harped repeatedly on **M** as a film with a social message (mandatory in most film communities is a politically correct message to confirm that activities such as rape, abduction and murder are not condoned by the authorities, nor society) about the importance of taking good care of children and as a film that stages a debate about the death penalty, he made one particularly telling off-hand observation about just what fascinated him about the serial murders of the 1920s. In following various cases in the newspapers, Lang was struck by the way in which the unsolved murders seemed almost automatically to foster what he described as a psychosis of fear ("Angstpsyhose") - for him, a revolting mentality that mingled misanthropy with overzealousness to produce the kind of behavior that led to the denunciation of neighbours and other associates (creating a mob mentality)." (Tatar)

It is as though the public yearns for an excuse to release hostility and hatred towards an acceptable icon which can only be found possible in situations such as serial killings. When little Elsie Beckmann, the child victimised in **M**, is murdered, the public all turns on each other, finding scapegoats in those that are "different" or simply unliked in day to day life, yet the killer is as much beyond all of them, as he is directly in front of them. By the end of the film the audience is manipulated into feeling sorry for the murderer, Mr. Beckert played by Peter Lorre. He is, we are led to believe, as much a victim of his "pain" and his "urges", as his victims are to his torment. It is a perfect example of how the subtle differences in the portrayal of heinous crime in cinema stand slightly apart between the beginning of the genre and now.

Despite whatever shock we may exhibit in studying the past of sex and murder in art and culture, we as a society now are still as fascinated and intrigued. There is something about that primordial taboo that cannot be denied. That fascination sells successful books and theater tickets. Audiences can't get enough of that which they are not supposed to have at all. In the American mainstream we see it in our own day and age. We don't have to travel back to Weimar. From independent films such as **Henry: Portrait of a Serial Killer** (1986) or mainstream blockbusters such as **Hannibal**, or the recent film of the life of Ed Gein, Americas first serial killer. When it comes to murder, we yearn for insight and enlightenment into those secret sins.

Continuing the passion in the underground, Barrel Entertainment offers us the modern contemporary journey into the mind of the serial killer with **Schramm** (1993), directed by Jorg Buttergereit, and even more taboo by the same director **Nekromantik** (1987) & **Nekromantik 2** (1991) which have sold out all copies at most of the stores carrying them!

"Erregung" for "Lustmord" and "Leibstod" are as much in demand today as the day the terms were first coined back in Weimar! Shock Cinema thrives on that which scares us all worse than monsters - - real life horror that could be waiting around any corner, the monster being someone you may very well know!

This essay appeared in *CineMuerte* magazine/film festival, Vancouver. B.C. Thanks Kier-La 7/01

This is a revised version of an academic annotation of work by Maria Tatar for Goddard College

The Killing Box

Steve Earles

The **Killing Box** is a film that tells its tale on a lyrical as well as visual level, both are afforded equal importance. Thus, the film begins by defining what *The Killing Box* is…

'The Killing Box is a term still used by the military today. It describes a manoeuvre in which an enemy unit is surrounded on both sides and massacred.'

'As a rule, no human soldier escapes the bloody horror of The Killing Box'.

'On December 28, on the banks of Catums Creek in Tennessee, the rule changed.'

In brisk economic strokes we know what a Killing Box is, what it does, and the time and place.

The visual impact of **The Killing Box** strikes dramatically with its images of crucified Union soldiers (one of whom is played by Matt LeBlanc, of *Friends tv* fame, in by-far his best acting performance, perhaps a directors cut of **The Killing Box** exists where the entire cast of *Friends* is crucified). As they are photographed, frozen in monochrome, we wonder what enemy could have done this? Inside the mouth of one of the dead union soldiers is a Confederate belt buckle bearing the legend 'Alabama 1st'.

Captain John Harling has served his time in the Union army. Educated and god-fearing, he serves his country for duty rather than glory, and while he is not a coward, he is glad to be done with the business of exterminating his fellow men. Harling is played by Adrian Pasdar, bringing the same quality to the role that he brought to the classic **Near Dark** (1987). But before he can resign his commission, he is called to the luxurious quarters of General Haworth, played by Martin Sheen. Haworth is a general who speaks of sacrifice while posing for his portrait (the painter

The Killing Box

is played by **The Killing Box**'s director George Hickenlooper, creating art within art). Haworth tells Harling he cannot resign his commission. He shows Harling photographs of the crucified soldiers. Harling is horrified, his one-time friend Colonel Nehemiah Strayn was commander of the Alabama 1st. Strayn had been mentor to Harling before the war, now he rots in a Union prison. Harling receives permission to take Strayn into his custody, who better to find the Alabama 1st than their leader.

Inside the hellish prison, Harling confronts Strayn (played with surprising strength and sensitivity by Corbin Bernsen). Strayn is confronted with the evidence of the belt buckle but cannot believe his men carried out the atrocity he sees in the photographs. For a very good reason......all his men are dead.

Trapped by Union soldiers in a Killing Box , a year earlier at Catums Creek, Strayn ordered his men to surrender. Having done so, the Yankees proceeded to massacre the Rebels. Strayn was the sole survivor. So, Strayn and Harling set out with a regiment of Union soldiers in search of the truth.

Meanwhile, we see what has been carrying out the killings. They look like confederate soldiers, but their faces are inhuman, painted in some tribal fashion alien to America. The special make-up effects from KNB are much more subtle than we would normally expect. They seem invulnerable to bullets and make short work of any opposition. With one exception, a slave girl who manages to escape them. She is the sole survivor when Harling and his men come across the scene to be confronted with the crucifixions they had only seen in sepia photographs. Hardened though they are to carnage, the reality of it disturbs them.

To his disgust, the racist Strayn finds himself chained to the slave girl. The friction between Harling and Strayn could be cut with a knife. Strayn is more than a match for any argument. He is like stone, rigid in his racist views, righteous in his belief that his men could not have done such a thing.

They return to Catums Creek to investigate the fate of Strayns regiment. Strayn dives into the water of the creek and enters a cave. There, he encounters his nephew, his regiment's drummer boy, who tells him his story. How the dead bodies of the slaughtered Alabama 1st were swept by the current to the cave, where they became... something else.

The Killing Box

Then, the drummer boy can no longer control the thing inside him and he bites Strayn, who escapes but surfaces from the creek more dead than alive.

Strayn is nursed back to health by the slave girl. As he recovers, he begins to change. He finds himself like a helpless child. His racism begins to dissolve. He discovers she is psychic. Even though she is mute, she tells him her name is Rebecca. She tells him much more as Strayn relates to Harling…

'A long while ago in Africa, there was a village. In it lived a very powerful tribe. No one ever dared tangle with them because everyone knew what they were guarding. Like that black cave back there at Catums Creek. Inside it… out of a nightmare. Years ago, the tribe had bottled those begins in that hole. They didn't want what was down there getting out, spreading their poison, consuming, making. Two hundred years ago, white slave traders came. They attacked the village. Killed the men. Took most of the women. One of the slavers had the bright idea of going down that hole. He found something alright, but it weren't slaves. He came out, he weren't just a slave-trader. That man brought a plague here, John, and a whole lot of people where changed like my men. Rebecca's ancestors where the ones that hunted them down and bottled 'em up in that cave I found. Rebecca's the only one left who knows how to end this.'

The Killing Box invites comparison with Hammer Films **Plague of the Zombies** (1966) and **The Reptile** (1966). Both films (shot back to back, using many of the same sets, and many of the same actors and crew) feature conflict involving an alien spiritual power in conflict with a western/Christian belief.

There are a number of other prominent themes in **The Killing Box**, for this is a film that works on a myriad of levels. There is the classic horror film theme 'revenge of the repressed'. The slaves stolen from Africa may have been killed, used and abused. But their takers have unwittingly released the seeds of their own destruction.

There is a theme of transformation. From human to something else. Colonel Strayn's transformation from arrogant racist.

There is a theme of conflict. Between North and South. Slave and master. Prisoner and jailer. Harling and Strayn. Strayn and the Union soldiers. All against the common enemy.

Neamiah gives Rebecca his fathers silver watch; "my daddy'd kill

Plague of the Zombies

me if he knew I gave my watch to a nig..nice girl like you." They also encounter some troops guarding a wagon. At their next encounter with the Alabama 1st, Rebecca uses the silver watch to ward off Strayns attacker, who while changed in body, isn't changed in mind, "you're a strong one, shame we don't take niggers."

Colonel Thalman has been bitten, dying, he fills in one of the missing pieces of the puzzle, "We were wrong about the crucifixions. They weren't trying to frighten us. They were trying to keep the weak ones from rising up. I have been a soldier all my days and would like to live my final moments in the company of my fellows."

Harling noticed they avoided the wagon. When he discovers its full of silver, he remembers Rebecca saving Strayn with a silver watch. Harling's narrative brings to mind the oral tradition of ghost stories that existed at that time. It has the dry lyrical quality of a tale by Poe or Twain.

"Stolen silver that has once adorned a family's dining table became ammunition for our rifles, a poison sheet for our bayonets. A simple trough of water was transformed from a tool of irrigation into an invincible line in the earth. Coin was turned from currency into an impervious walls. I could not fathom how any of there could fend off such a ruthless enemy. Military logic had begun to fade with the waning daylight, making less clear the lines between blue and gray, black and white, sanity and insanity. I could only now pray the winds of fate would be merciful to us all and carry us to a place where lies undivided ground, and Strayn himself had elected to become human bait. A lure into what would be the most bizarre *Killing Box* in military history."

Silver is the traditional bane of evil. Harling later refers to it as 'the most expensive battle of the war." Strayn confronts his former comrades in the *Killing Box*. In common with **Near Dark**, the creatures are not named. They don't need a name. They know what they are and it scarcely matters to their victims. Perhaps by naming what they are would dilute the terror. Less is more.

They appeal; to Strayn, "Nehemiah, we're your brothers", to no avail, the evil is sterilized by silver. In the ultimate act of self-sacrifice, Rebecca gives her life to save Strayn.

The Killing Box ends as it began, the photographer shoots the aftermath. Strayn hangs the silver watch on the plain cross that marks Rebecca's grave. Harling tries to comfort him, "She was brave, Sir." Strayn replies grimly. "Braver than you know." Harlings narrative concludes **The Killing Box**.

" On that day, I, John Laurence Harling, released my former mentor from captivity and thus forfeited my discharge. I was forced to remain on active duty. As a result I will be serving under General Ulysses S Grant until the end of the war. Nehemiah Pearson Stryan rejoined the Confederate army and was to serve valiantly at the battles of Gettysburg, Chickamauga and Cole Harbour. Though still an ardent believer in the Southern cause, he made many enemies due to his outspoken stance against slavery. After the war it is rumoured he returned to the cave at Catums Creek to rescue his nephew, the last remaining member of his regiment. To my knowledge, he has not been heard of ...."

BECOMING-MONSTER: DELEUZE AND THE ANOMALIES OF HORROR

Anna Powell

Alone in his bathroom, Seth Brundle watches himself in the mirror Anxiously scanning his increasingly knobbly face, he chews his fingernail and it comes off between his teeth. His exposed finger end squirts white liquid all over the mirror, which he shamefacedly wipes off with toilet paper. The next scene in David Cronenberg's **The Fly** (1986) begins with a slow track up the solid metal of a computer, panning round to reveal Seth at the screen. Instead of providing him with reassurance, what he sees on the screen intensifies the horror. Analysing the cellular makeup of Seth's teleportation, the computer reveals that the secondary element in the genetic mix is "not-Brundle". With mounting terror and disgust, Seth scans blown-up images of hairy spikes and the text reveals a "fusion of Brundle and Fly at a molecular level".

This chapter uses Gilles Deleuze and Felix Guattari's concept of becoming to trace the transformations of horror film characters into hybrids of human and not-human. Humans who become monsters are a basic motif of horror film, which gleefully deploys effects technology such as prosthetic makeup and computer-generated imagery to manifest monstrosity. The viewer also delights in these bodily changes which we experience with a potent mix of revulsion and fascination. A favourite locus for spectacular bodily modification is the transgression of biological and cultural gender norms. I would like to explore the anomalies of gender in the horror film, and situate the mutating forms of masculinity and femininity within the process of becoming.

To pinpoint the intersection between singularities, or self-referential systems, Gilles Deleuze and Felix Guattari use the figure of the "Anomalous". Anomalies are unnatural, irregular elements in a system. Deleuze's description of them references the creatures of dark fantasy and horror in literature. He writes:

the Anomalous is always at the frontier, on the border of a band or a multiplicity; it is part of the latter, but it is already making it pass into another multiplicity, it makes it become, it traces a line-between. This is also the "outsider". Moby Dick, or the Thing or Entity of Lovecraft, terror."

Men who become monsters, men who become women, and women who become other life-forms are anomalies in horror cinema, and the objects of our fascination. Essentialist associations of women with irrationality, insatiable urges and occult powers make them susceptible to monstrous transformations. Even if they are not themselves monsters, they side with the monster in its otherness to patriarchal power. The elision of woman and predatory animals motivates such films as **The Reptile** (John Gilling, 1966) **Cat People** (Jacques Tourneur, 1943) and the **Alien** series. Despite attempts to restore order at the end of many horror films, female and male mutants undermine cultural attempts to maintain self-consistent gender norms.

FILM THEORY CHANGES FACE

There is already a substantial body of work on representations of women in horror film, both as victim and monster. Among the key perspectives are those of culturalism (Carol Clover) and psychoanalysis (Barbara Creed).

The Reptile

Silence of the Lambs

These approaches, foundational to feminist horror film studies, identify the operations of misogyny or read active female characters in a politically progressive way. Psychoanalysis locates the monster in the Oedipal mix of desire and dread. Repressed energies, released by the violation of taboos, return in monstrous form. Monstrous women, particularly vampires, have been celebrated as transgressive.

As well as textual readings, Clover presents the viewing process itself as subverting gender norms, discovering male masochism in rape-revenge and slasher movie audiences. These abjection/transgression–based approaches are underpinned by the binary dynamic of the norm and its other. Their hegemony in feminist horror criticism may be challenged by a model that moves away from binarities. As well as challenging the psychoanalytic account of subject-formation, this approach repudiates any simple elision of representation and reality.

The predominance of Laura Mulvey's theory of the gaze in feminist film studies, based on Lacanian psychoanalysis and French film criticism, is undermined by Deleuzian approaches. Rather than the masterful detachment of the gaze, our whole body participates in the event of the film as part of the flux of the material world in what Guattari calls "affective contamination". The vibrations of light and colour, sound, texture and movement engage us in force and sensation prior to figurative representations and narrative patterns. The visceral experience of the viewer's mind/brain/body rather than the deep structures of the subjective unconscious operate as part of the "machinic assemblage" of cinema. We participate in a wider formation of assemblages connected in their turn to the apparatus of cinema. This includes technology, economics, politics, aesthetics and their attendant relations of power.

Deleuze and Guattari develop the concept of becoming (the infinitive *devenir*), the continual process of movement and flux. They build on its use in Nietzsche, who uses the term throughout his work for the dynamic metamorphosis of matter, and human potential. The philosophy of Bergson, who speaks of "that continuity of becoming which is reality itself" is another source. In becoming, subject/object boundaries meld together in molecular fusion to form a new entity. If we open up to potential transformations, we experience other ways of being in the world. Our perceptions must be ready for the challenge of a fresh perspective, in which we acknowledge our molecular continuity with other existences. We can fuse perceptually and imaginatively with both organic and inorganic matter.

In their discussion of becoming, Deleuze and Guattari suggest that molecularity underpins the makeup of all matter and enables us to make multiple, "rhizomatic" (a bifurcating root-system) connections. They write that "all becomings are molecular: the animal, flower or stone one becomes are molecular collectivities, haecceities, not molar subjects, objects or forms that we know from the outside and recognise from experience, through science or by habit". They extend their discussion of becoming-animal to include the mutations and hybrids of myth. Folk tales of shape-shifting suggest that the boundaries of humans and other life-forms are not fixed, but that molecular flows conjoin separate species:

Man does not become wolf, or vampire, as if he changed molar species; the vampire and the werewolf are becomings of man, in other words, proximities between molecules in composition, relations of movement and rest, speed and slowness between emitted particles. Of course there are werewolves and vampires...

Vampires, werewolves and other hybrids image human affinities with beasts, plants and minerals. We may connect with other singularities via common organic processes and speeds of flow. Rather than losing our specificity, or being swamped by melding, we expand to take in the anomalous, like the protozoa often cited by Deleuze.

Singularities are connected by "lines of flight", which open up connecting channels for fluid exchanges. The "deterritorialisation" offered by such becoming extends to cultural experiences such as film watching. The apparatus of cinema presents virtual objects to spectators, so film's direct ability to represent material reality is inevitably limited. It produces flattened, abstracted and partial copies of objects from the outset. Rather than seeking a mirrored reality in cinema, we respond more rewardingly to the sensory stimuli of the apparatus and its affective impact. If we become absorbed in the experience of film, it may alter and extend our more mundane modes of consciousness.

In Deleuze's classification, the "movement image" of action-oriented feature films appeals to our sensory-motor capacities, and the "time-image" is manifest in more experimental forms like Italian Neo-Realism and the work of Godard. These works enable the contemplation of philosophical issues like time and duration. Despite the small number of films and directors in the Deleuzian canon of the time-image, he does cite a wider range in the movement-image, including populist director such as Hitchcock. Mainstream Hollywood generally fits the movement-image paradigm. Exceptions to this are found in the work of maverick directors such as Welles who, with Greg Toland, introduced the aesthetic innovations of deep focus admired by André Bazin.

A shift to Deleuze in film studies is underway as part of a broad rethinking of aesthetics in contemporary culture. Reflecting scientific and philosophical issues of space and time, relativity, quantum mechanics and molecular biology, it shifts focus from the "molar" politics of representation to the "molecular" materiality of film. Following Henri Bergson, Deleuze argues that identity is in constant flux and process. Perception takes place on a direct, visceral level in what Barbara Kennedy calls a "pathic, proto-subjective state which is not owned by the subject". If our subjectivity is not fixed, then our gender identity in the viewing experience is not a rigid template, but a fluid becoming.

BECOMING-WOMAN

Within this changing theoretical map, issues of gender and its

Psycho

representation might seem to be erased. They are, however, still relevant to our understanding of becoming and its potential to change experiential events and empirical reality.   Feminist theorists have found Deleuze's work both exasperating and stimulating. There is now a substantial critical discussion of his terminology by Camilla Griggers, Elizabeth Grosz and others. They have used Deleuze's work as a constructive set of tools to shape new directions in feminist thought. The concept of becoming has been applied to a rethinking of the position of women in contemporary culture.

Deleuze's comments on becoming-woman have been attacked by some feminist critics. They appear to be deliberately couched in essentialist terms that associate woman with nature in "springs and flows" and "becoming-animal".   In his defence, Deleuze argues that "Nature, matter, affection and passion are not here perceived as static or negative terms, but are flowing and relational, changing and creative, and so their connotations in relation to "woman" no longer have their earlier connotations of otherness". He refutes gender "binary machines" in favour

Dressed To Kill

of the molecular and fluid sexuality of "a thousand tiny sexes". Becoming-woman indicates a more general destabilisation of identity because woman is the other of the norm, man. In the same way he uses the figure of the girl as the other of woman thus doubly subverting the male norm. Men can become-woman, whilst both women and men can form assemblages with other singularities, to continue their own becoming.

From a philosophical perspective, Grosz writes that "becoming-woman means going beyond identity and subjectivity, fragmenting, freeing up lines of flight". Griggers offers provocative culturalist applications of the term in her book Becoming Woman in which she considers the transmutations of woman in contemporary experience. Griggers describes the various non-human assemblages that modern women are connected to, using Guattari's term "abstract-machine":

Woman is an abstract-machine concretely produced by late-twentieth-century technologies and capital. Her forms of expression are determined by optical and electronic media, psychopharmacology, the war machine, the chemical industry, plastics technology, bioscience."

Griggers makes political and social use of becoming-woman to explore the problematics of feminism and its need to respond to rapidly changing cultures, both internationally and in the USA.

BODIES WITHOUT ORGANS

Further light may be shed on Deleuze's concept of becoming by his deployment of the Body Without Organs (BWO), a term borrowed from Artaud who used it as an emblem of bodily transformation. For Deleuze, the BWO seeks a denaturalisation of the biological body , a widening of the meanings of the term body, and an equalisation of all forms of body. He shares Spinoza's belief in the univocity of being, by which all matter, being made up of patterns of particles and fibres, shares the same ontological status, Male and female BWOs have mutated beyond fixed gender oppositions. They can potentially connect with all other bodies to form new assemblages.

As well as organic bodies, there are technological and cultural

Dressed To Kill

bodies. Film is a process of BWOs, as the bodies of apparatus, text and spectator operate in conjunction. Cinema intersects physiology and psychology with technological apparatus in an immanent process. A potent affective experience is produced which, at its most powerful, accesses spiritual dimensions. This assemblage, which operates on the material plane, may also embody metaphysical concepts, such as space, movement and duration. Deleuze writes that "it is through the body (and no longer through the intermediary of the body) that cinema forms its alliance with spirit, with thought". Cinema, at what he considers to be its best, is a highly prized route for lines of flight to pass between bodies.

Deleuze's work contains little direct reference to the horror film. Classic realist texts such as Hollywood horror films are not regarded by him as vehicles for existential change. It is likely that horror films are excluded because of their explicit imagery and predilection for formulaic narrative structure and continuity editing. Deleuze prefers parametric, art-house narration, avant-garde visual style and non-continuity editing, as

Dressed To Kill

more suited to stimulate philosophical thought in the viewer. I will argue, however, that much can be gained by Deleuzian applications to horror film. In particular, the concept of becoming makes suggestive inroads into the hybridisation of men, women and monsters.

After melding with a stray fly in the teleporter, he behaves like a pre-pubescent boy gorging on chocolate bars and throwing tantrums (becoming-boy would presumably be positioned by Deleuze as even worse than the masculine norm). Rather than his usual nerdy persona, Brundle degenerates further into machismo. This is evident in pointless displays of strength as he smashes a wooden beam in the lab and strides downtown bare-chested beneath his leather jacket. He breaks an opponent's arm in an arm wrestling match and practically drags a woman in the bar back to his lab for casual sex. The male mad scientist is revealed as unworthy of the powers he wields. Like others of his ilk, Seth is punished for hubristic meddling with the laws of nature. His arrogant male molecules are subject to a humiliating fusion with those of an insect associated with lechery and dirt.

If we shift focus from a negative gender reading to open up other elements in **The Fly**, both Brundle-Fly's agenda and the ending may be interpreted differently. Leaving human constraints behind, he revels in his new formation. His evolutionary drives seek further development of the hybrid species. Brundle-Fly ostensibly wants Veronica to fuse with him to dilute his fly genes, but further hybridisation could occur (visualised as a monstrous maggot in her birth dream). His destruction by his own teleporter by a "normal" male rival for Veronica removes the threat he posed to biological security. He challenges both fantasies of subjective autonomy and species purity. Brundle-Fly presents a radical model of becoming that undermines essentialist norms. He accepts the need to adapt to his new assemblage and become-fly. Other types of men becoming-monster have adapted less well their chosen assemblage and return us to the problematics of gender difference.

DRESSING TO KILL

Deleuze draws an important distinction between molecular becoming and copying. He notes that "all becomings are already molecular. This is because becoming is not to imitate or identify with someone". Men may sometimes copy women in horror film, adopting a superficial masquerade of femininity by wearing items of women's clothing, wigs and makeup. This cross-dressing may be an indicator of social deviance, as with Buffalo Bill in **Silence of the Lambs** (Jonathan Demme, 1991). Schizophrenia and psychotic breakdown may also deploy transvestite identification like the Oedipal mother figure projected and performed by Norman Bates in **Psycho** (Alfred Hitchcock, 1960). The unmasking of gender disguise forms a grotesque climax in Brian DePalma's **Dressed to Kill** (1980).

The sympathetic and troubled psychiatrist Dr. Robert Elliott is revealed as a transvestite/transsexual killer of women. The final dénouement, in flashes of blue light as a storm rages outside, is made by a slow track up his wounded body. Beginning with black stockings and stilettos, it lingers on the incongruity of his square jaw and craggy features with the long blonde wig lying on the floor. His own analyst later reveals that Elliott blamed the murder of a client, Mrs. Miller on "Barbie", his feminine alter-ego. Like Norman Bates, sexual arousal leads Elliott not to repression but to schizoid splitting and repudiation of responsibility.

The pseudo-becomings of these schizophrenic men parody feminine accoutrements by imitation and are deeply misogynistic, enabling under-cover serial murders of women. Jerry Aline Flieger comments on the well-known case-study of Judge Schreber's schizoid deployment of a female role in fantasy. She notes that the skewed imitation of becoming-woman can be used "a means to an end for man, however "real" is Schreber's "virtual" experience of womanhood", merely fulfilling the agenda of a disturbed male. Both Bates and Elliott remain Freudian case-studies rather than Deleuze/Guattarian becoming-women.

Further along the line towards becoming-woman is a molecular melding of gender which is only temporary. In the Hammer film **Dr. Jekyll and Sister Hyde** (1971), it lasts until the drug wears off. The transformation behind the locked doors of Jekyll's lab depends not on prosthetics but on the casting of Martine Beswick for her physical resemblance to Ralph Bates (long black hair, dark eyes, sharp cheekbones). The manifestation of a female double enables Jekyll and his "sister" to seduce the wholesome biological brother and sister upstairs. It also offers the possibly masturbatory pleasures of narcissism, as when the newly transformed sister caresses his/her breasts in the mirror. Like Jack the Ripper, Hyde stabs prostitutes to death and uses his/her gender change as a mask to deceive the police.

Dr. Jekyll and Sister Hyde

Sister Hyde chiefly murders women, as does Norman Bates, Robert Elliott and Buffalo Bill. "Phallic" guns and knives, revealed from beneath feminine clothes and brandished, are the weapons of choice. Transsexual and transvestite monsters hide behind the assumption that women would not be capable of the brutality that a feminine disguise allows the man.

None of these murderers successfully become-woman because they retain their misogynistic masculine agendas. They remain closet men and fail to open up their masculinity to a molecular meld with the other. The visual and aural performance of womanhood is fetishised by glamorous clothes, makeup, wigs and high-pitched voices. Such masquerade provides horror film with fascinating mileage. The masculine interior beneath the feminine surface adds a struggle for precedence to the plot dynamics. In a sense, the monster is the man who finally shows his face. A more subversive take on becoming-woman in terms of both imagery and plot can be seen in Cronenberg's **Videodrome** (1982).

In Cronenberg's vision of "the new flesh", mutation at a molecular level leads to objects becoming flesh and flesh becoming machine. Stephen Shaviro suggests that in Cronenberg's work, biotechnology is used to convey a troublingly plastic ambiguity, which is oppositional to the ideology of dominant cinema. He argues that:

"By insisting on the gross palpability of the flesh, and by heightening (instead of minimising) our culture's pervasive discomfort with materiality, Cronenberg opposes the way in which dominant cinema captures, polices, and regulates desire, precisely by providing sanitised models of fulfilment."

In **Videodrome**, a video cassette box appears to become woman, growing mammary bulges. The Videodrome tape has the capacity to cause cellular mutations in its hosts. As media guru Brian O'Blivion announces "the visions became flesh, uncontrollable flesh". The molecular malformation of brain cells manifest itself in altered states of consciousness, which the viewer as well as the characters finds increasingly difficult to differentiate from empirical reality. Max Renn is a producer for a pornographic cable TV channel and Nicki Brand is a radio chat show host with masochistic sexual tastes. When they begin an affair, Max's intense involvement with Nicky, which involves submitting to her demands for pain, leads to his own increasing permeability to change. His fear, desire and wonder take

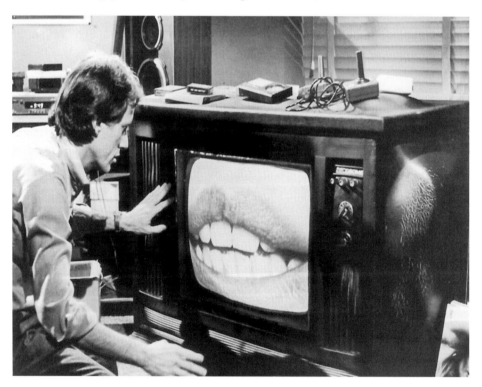

Videodrome

on increasingly physical manifestations, ranging from subtle shifts in facial expression and body language to extravagant hallucinations.

When the villainous Barry Convex tries to make Max "open up" to the power of *Videodrome*, he thrusts the cassette into a vagina-like orifice which opens up in Max's torso after his shirt buttons have popped. This male/male/female penetration scene with its perverse eroticism is redolent with Freudian potential, but goes beyond the merely sexual. Max experiences the insertion as violation and his conscious mind is outraged by it. Shortly afterwards, he opens his own gut up to retrieve a gun that he had previously inserted into the slit. The gun emerges, dripping with white ejaculate-like liquid. In a painfully tactile sequence, the weapon penetrates Max's hand, growing metal roots into his flesh like a parasitic organic life form, with insectlike tentacles piercing the flesh. The sequence features close-ups of Max's outraged, anxious and gratified face. As well as these visual images, the uncanny nature of his becomings is heightened aurally by the sound of wind and ominous electronic chords on the soundtrack.

High angle shots of Max crawling along the floor in pain and humiliation underlines his growing masochistic congruence with Nicki. For Shaviro, Max's transformation "demonstrates gender as a social construction of the body" and "absurdly, hyperbolically links the ideology that equates femininity with passivity, receptivity, and castration". On one level, Max has "become" Nicki, but at the same time, he has also opened up what Deleuze calls "a thousand tiny sexes" in himself. This permeability results from his passing through the boundaries of the human as he melds with metal, plastic and other non-organic substances. The film illustrates Deleuze's becoming-woman by Max's openness to his own mutation. This process only partially liberates him from rigid boundaries. Max's becomings are enforced in a sinister plot to manipulate reality by warping minds. Despite his developing psychological and emotional complexity, he sinks into despair and kills himself. The horror genre requires him to be destroyed by his very openness to becoming as well as his erotic deviance.

THE BEAST IN WOMAN

Deleuze recommends becoming-woman as a useful device to subvert the rigid norms of patriarchy. Biological women are also able to become-

Videodrome

woman, or become-girl, just as they can become-animal or make a variety of other assemblages. This involves stepping outside the construct of "woman" as man's opposite in binary structure. In horror cinema, women's becomings are represented as more "natural" and less of a violently enforced change than the correspondingly flamboyant masculine mutations. There is generally less focus on the changeover process itself in terms of action and mise-en-scène. With Norman Bates, Dr. Elliott and Dr. Jekyll, apparently normal masculinity is stressed prior to transvestite performance. When women become beasts, we are presented with their anomalies as fait accompli. This is due to prior coding of their physical appearance and behaviour as laden with signifiers of bestiality. It may also be connected to a racialised otherness.

In **Cat People**, bestial becomings are foregrounded from the start. The woman/panther Irena (Simone Simon) is feline in appearance, with snub nose and tilted eyes. She makes slinky movements in her flowing black gowns and furs, and gazes up to men with wide-eyed, kittenish charm. She is rendered doubly other by her Eastern European origins. In a heavily accented voice, she recounts her ominous tale of the Serbian legend of the Cat People and the ancestral curse of women who change into feline predators when their passions are aroused. Irena feels more affinity with the panthers in the zoo than her fellow humans and obsessively sketches them. A statue of King John slaying a demonic feline dominates her apartment.

Irena's becoming-monster is presented as a sudden, irrational shift of mood when her passions (specifically desire and jealousy) are aroused. The mechanics of her transformation into the panther are concealed by the subtle stylistic techniques of this low-budget horror film (unlike the more overt re-make by Paul Schrader, 1981). Tourneur's film includes the expressionistic use of dreams, shadow-play and intercutting between Irena and the panther. Shots of paw marks becoming footprints underline the magical ease of the transmutation.

Despite the affinity built up between woman and beast, real animals, especially cats, are terrified by Irena. At the same time, she behaves like a cat herself, squeezing a pet canary to death and clawing the sofa. In the zoo at night, she savages sheep. The film plays on traditional associations of woman, cats and witchcraft and aligns female passion (specifically desire and jealousy) with regressive, bestial becoming. The chief focus of her

Videodrome

attacks is a potential rival for her husband's affections. Psychoanalysis vies with the occult to explain the events, but is finally discredited. Irena claws her analyst to death after embracing him, in his just deserts for unprofessional conduct.

The film's presentation of becoming-cat is deeply ambivalent. Irena is a melancholy and alluring figure whose human desires are unable to maintain the control needed to repress her animal nature. Her death may be viewed as the punishment for several crimes against acceptable femininity. She has frustrated her husband and transferred her desire to the analyst. She has acted in an unsisterly way to her husband's friend, ripping her robe and terrifying her by becoming-panther at the pool. Aligned with nature, she is also unnatural. As well as being the victim of a curse, she is a sinister and untrustworthy foreigner, unlike the all-American workmate who her husband finally goes off with.

The Hammer film **The Reptile** again aligns foreignness with female monstrosity and reflects tensions and phobias about Asian immigration in the mid 1960s in fantasy form. Prior to being identified as *The Reptile*, Anna Franklin (Jacqueline Pearce) is already presented as an exotic creature, anomalous in the Cornish landscape. Anna is an ethnic hybrid of genes from her colonial English father and nameless Malaysian mother. She is sinuous, slender and dark, and hypnotises her guests into trance by her magical sitar playing. The physical and moral degeneracy of her "mixed blood" is contrasted to the wholesome, blonde "English rose" Mrs. Spalding who mistakenly seeks to befriend her. Anna's bestial affinities are evident in her obsession with animals and birds kept in cages as pets, but secretly devoured. Lacking autonomous agency, she is dominated by two sinister men, her stern father and the Malaysian man-servant who controls her transformations by hypnotism. There is no gradual melding of two entities as with **The Fly**, when Seth retains elements of his personality and physical features almost until the end. The prosthetics department fitted Anna with a ludicrous bug-eyed mask for her appearance as *The Reptile* and she is completely unrecognisable apart from her frock.

For these suspect foreign women who become monsters, membership of the human species is itself presented as a masquerade which they have difficulty in maintaining. As both foreign and female, they have inherent monster potential and can easily "turn" or regress genetically. Like other monsters, Irena and Anna are products of the ideological prejudices and sexual anxieties of their cultural context. A more recent image of woman's becoming-monster is the anomalous status of Ripley (Sigourney Weaver) in Jean-Pierre Jeunet's **Alien Resurrection** (1997).

SHARING SPECIES: ALIEN RESURRECTION

In his study of Melville's novel *Moby Dick* Deleuze indicates that the whale as well as Ahab must become in order for their molecular assemblage to operate fully. Successful becomings are mutual arrangements between congruent parties. They do not necessarily require a matching two-way interchange and each party retains its specificity. Singularities are free to make any number of subsequent connections. **Alien Resurrection** can be viewed as a becoming-monster in which the monster also becomes-human.

As with Cronenberg's films, becomings take place at a cellular level here, and like the fusion of **The Fly**, they are initially engineered by scientists. In Jeunet's film, the scientists serve their employers, United Systems Military, unquestioningly. Surrendering ethical considerations, they have used genetic engineering ruthlessly to clone cells from Ripley prior to her self-immolation (At the end of **Alien 3** she kills herself to avoid hosting an embryonic alien). Their inhumane experiments have already cloned several abortive hybrids of the two genetic strands. Some aliens have human genes and one fully functional Ripley has alien genes.

The scientists are themselves the most monstrous beings on the ship. In the mad scientist mould, they are condemned for playing God. Becomings should by rights be assemblages of consensus and collective agency. Here, they have been enforced, and the existential rights of the singularities involved denied, causing terrible suffering. The film locates emotional depth with semi, rather than fully, human characters. In a harrowing scene, one of the clones used for the enforced breeding of an alien demands the right to die and Ripley mercifully torches her. Another scientifically engineered hybrid, the android, Call, develops emotional complexity and an uneasy friendship with Ripley.

The ethos of fluid identity in the film has been read by Catherine Constable who sets up Ripley as the "intersection point" for several life-systems. Constable draws on Christine Battersby's work with Irigaray's model of permeable feminine boundaries. This valorises patterns of flow

Alien Resurrection

in which the body itself "becomes a permeable structure, a volume without contours, whose physical fluidity sustains and supports the possibilities of intimate embraces with others". In the film's opening scene, Constable notes how the figures of Ripley, Newt and the alien queen intersect in the morphing figure trapped in a glass tube. She uses birth as "a paradigm for re-thinking identity formation", but I want to move on from Constable's Irigarayan approach. Creed and Constable both read the Alien films from maternal perspectives based on the feminist psychoanalysis of Kristeva and Irigaray. Rather than taking up this theme again, I will look at other forms of melding in the fusion of congruent singularities.

The Ripley we see in **Alien Resurrection** is no longer so bounded by "woman" as a figure of gender difference as in the earlier films. The character is used rather to signal species difference, being neither fully human nor fully alien but sharing characteristics of both. When the ship lands on Earth at the end, she is left with potential for future becomings (and we are set up for another sequel). Our clear-cut identification with Ripley as hero in the previous films is undermined. We are no longer sure of her nature, her powers or her agenda. **Alien Resurrection** conveys a strong mutual desire for reconnection between the artificially spliced blocs, Alien and Ripley, drawing them irrevocably together. This is foregrounded in a sequence where Ripley is taken to witness the alien birth.

RIPLEY'S RELATIVES

From the outset, Ripley is both more than and other than human. From her genetic meld with the aliens, she has gained superhuman strength and corrosive blood. Her senses are preternaturally acute. On the run with the pirate gang, Ripley suddenly bends on all fours and snuffs the air like a beast. She is able to hear the alien's approach as the camera takes a 360 degree turn that emphasises her fluid movements and beast-like body-language. An alien opens the grating, so that she falls through onto its body below. We see her in long-shot wallowing with luxuriant abandon in a sea of tentacles. These resemble writhing rats' tails of a dark brown glistening wetness with abject, excremental associations. She is briefly engulfed as the mass pulses in and out, then she emerges to spread her limbs with easy confidence. Without fear, she sinks into it by folding up her arms with a rhythm and speed corresponding to those of the pulsing mass.

My position as a viewer is partly informed by an identification with Ripley built up in the previous films. This affinity is complicated here by her ready embrace of abjection. Even though parallels are drawn earlier between Ripley and the aliens in **Alien**, **Aliens** and **Alien 3**, the inevitable confrontations and show-downs depend on a dynamic of polarity. In this film, the aliens are humanised and Ripley becomes more overtly alien herself as the species meld on several levels. Constable reads the subsequent embrace as sexual intercourse because Ripley lies beneath the male creature, but I would question this interpretation because the male alien is a drone in service of the queen.

The embrace in which the alien carries Ripley to the queen is both repellent and attractive. The special status of the sequence is enhanced by the use of strobe- lighting during the journey and by stirring incidental music with drum rolls and horns playing a lyrical melody. These effects combine with slow editing rhythms to enhance a sense of timelessness as the two beings embrace. Time is extended by three long-held shots, similarly composed, in which Ripley lies beneath him and is cradled and caressed. Rather than sexual intercourse, this suggests a blissful moment of species recognition and melding, or familial bonding. Medium close-ups, which serve to increase our sense of intimate engagement, show Ripley's appearance as distinctly human. Her facial expression is blissful and serene. The alien has a blunt eyeless head with a protuberance resembling an insect's proboscis. Because we do not see its whole body, we are unsure of his exact size, shape or form. Whatever he looks like, Ripley appears to be at home in the alien milieu and is happy to meld with him. This apparent congeniality dilutes our revulsion.

The scene is Deleuzian in several ways. First, the "speeds and slownesses" of different life-forms are emphasised. The alien moves at a different pace and in a different duration to the human, but Ripley easily co-ordinates her movements with his, which assists the fusion. Unusual in the context of mainstream Hollywood, the sequence is wordless, with

Alien Resurrection

silent non-verbal communication and deep rapport. This segment, which stands out as stylistically distinct from the body of the film, suggests the operation of what Deleuze calls "opsigns" and "sonsigns". These are pure optical and/or sound situations that break from the narrative drive of the movement/action image to produce a "moment of pure contemplation" for the spectator.

The subsequent image shifts to an external long shot of the ship. This type of shot is often used as a form of punctuation in science fiction cinema. The image emphasises the vessel's hard metal casing and serves to return us to familiar boundaries. It re-establishes space, texture and shape and functions as "a breath of fresh air" after the cloying intimacy of the previous scene. After the punctuation, we return to the ship's hold, where Ripley lies wet, slimy and relaxed in the birth chamber. Her appearance suggests that she herself has undergone a form of birthing, in the acknowledgement of her own amorphous nature. In a parallel process, the alien baby is becoming-human. Rather than the bestial/insectoid appearance of the queen, the young alien has a familiarly humanoid skull, torso, teeth and deep blue eyes. It is this human coding which will further complicate our feelings when Ripley decides to destroy the infant for the sake of human survival.

BECOMING MONSTER AND THE DYNAMICS OF HORROR

Alien Resurrection approaches Deleuzian becoming more closely than the other examples of mutation we considered. It has moved on from the need to set up a polarised dynamic of norms and their transgression, whether by anomalous cross-dressing or molecular mutation. I wish to conclude by raising some questions about the future potential of horror/dark fantasy film if it were to continue along the "lines of flight" mapped out by **Alien Resurrection**. The first concerns issues of gender and representation. The character of Ripley is celebrated as the first feminist hero of substance in a predominantly masculinist genre. If she has become more of an alien than a human woman, the film could be adopting a more post-feminist position, with implications for the oppositional macro-politics of representation. Ripley does, however, remain an inspirational figure for becoming-woman. She had already adapted to becoming-alien and is ready for further transformations.

A further question concerns the future development of the affective dynamics of horror. If the monster and the human hero meld and form hybrids, the feelings usually roused by horror (fear, disgust, desire) are not mobilised in the same way. The horrific impact of the monster traditionally depends on its coding as anomalous, against nature in some sense. Becomings themselves are positioned as the source of horror. According to Kristeva's concept of abjection, the other functions to uphold, whilst contesting, human ethical and cultural norms. The monster terrifies us with the threat of subjective dissolution by infectious contact in tandem with an ambivalent desire to meld with it. Narrative closure often involves the monster's suppression and the re-instatement of diegetic norms. Although the alien infant is destroyed, our admiration for Ripley's resolve is mixed with outrage that she has killed her own "grandchild". Some of the horror and abjection are now attached to the hero herself

The current ideological and social climate is changing at an unprecedented rate. It adopts chaotic patterns as science, technology, economics and politics morph into new forms daily. Genetic engineering and viral mutations modify the existential and epistemological meaning of identity. "Man" and "woman" already conjoin with other singularities as well as with each other, adapting and taking on new formations of identity in the process. Cultural change breeds aesthetic innovation, which in its turn inputs into our affective experiences and our thoughts. The horror film and its monsters are part of this flux and are ripe for new becomings. Deleuze and Guattari's perspective embraces the anomalous to the point of fusing with it to form new assemblages. Part of this process, shared by character and spectator, is becoming-monster.

WORKS CITED

Bergson, Henri, *Matter and Memory*, trans. N. Margaret Paul and W. Scott Palmer, New York: Urzone, 1991.

Constable, Catherine, "Becoming the Alien's Mother: Morphologies of Identity in the Alien Series", in Annette Kuhn (ed) *Alien Zone II*, London and New York: Verso.

Clover, Carol, *Men, Women and Chainsaws: Gender in the Modern Horror Film*, London: BFI, 1992.

Creed, Barbara, *The Monstrous Feminine: Women in the Horror Film*, Manchester: Manchester University Press, 1993.

Deleuze, Gilles and Felix Guattari, *A Thousand Plateaus: Capitalism and Schizophrenia*, trans. R. Hurley, M. Seem, and H. R. Lane, London: Athlone, 1984.

Deleuze, Gilles and Claire Parnet, *Dialogues II*, London, New York: Continuum, 2002.

Deleuze, Gilles, *Cinema 2: The Time-Image*, trans. H. Tomlinson and R. Galeta, London: Athlone, 1995.

Deleuze, Gilles and Claire Parnet, *Dialogues*, trans. H. Tomlinson and B. Habberjam, London: Athlone, 1987.

Deleuze, Gilles and Claire Parnet, *Dialogues II*, London and New York: Continuum, 1992.

Fleiger, Jerry Ann, "Becoming-Woman: Deleuze, Schreber and Molecular Identification", in Ian Buchanan and Claire Colebrook (eds), *Deleuze and Feminist Theory*, Edinburgh: Edinburgh University Press, 2000.

Griggers, *Camilla Becoming-Woman: Theory Out of Bounds*, Minneapolis, University of Minnesota Press, 1997.

Grosz, Elizabeth, "A Thousand Tiny Sexes: Feminism and Rhizomatics", in Claire Boundas and Dorothy Olkowski (eds) *Gilles Deleuze and the Theatre of Philosophy*, London: Routledge, 1994.

Guattari, Felix, *Chaosmosis: An Ethico-Aesthetic Paradigm*, trans. P. Bains and J. Pefanis, Sidney: Power Publications, 1995.

Halberstam, Judith, *Skin Shows: Gothic Horror and the Technology of Monsters*, Durham and London: Duke University Press, 1995.

Kennedy, Barbara, *Deleuze and Cinema: The Aesthetics of Sensation*, Edinburgh: Edinburgh University Press, 2000.

Powell, Anna *Psychoanalysis and Sovereignty in Popular Vampire Fictions*, Lampeter: Mellen Press, 2003.

Shaviro, Steven, *The Cinematic Body*, University of Minnesota, Minneapolis, 1993.

Weiss, Andrea, *Vampires and Violets: Lesbians in the Cinema*, London: Jonathan Cape, 1992.

Williams, Linda "When the Woman Looks", in Mary Anne Doane, Patricia Mellencamp and Linda Williams (eds). *Re-vision: Essays in Feminist Film Criticism*, Frederick, Maryland: American Film Studies Monograph Series, University Publications of America, 1983.

Judith Halberstam, *Skin Shows: Gothic Horror and the Technology of Monsters*, Durham and London: Duke University Press, 1995.

Wish You Weren't Here? – Holidays in Hell

Andy Black

"Right now Americans feel unsafe in their own country… that's what **Hostel** *plays on – the American fear of other nationalities and their obnoxious, misplaced superiority."*

"There's no doubt in my mind **Hostel** *was a hit in America because it plays on the xenophobia of a nation where only ten percent of the population has a passport."*

Eli Roth – Director of **Hostel** (2005) and **Hostel 2** (2007).

"It's a cautionary tale, not about going to Brazil, but about travelling without any sort of research, without any sort of awareness about where you're from or what country you represent, and what may be the political climate that you're not aware of. That's what the movie is telling you to be cautious about."

Olivia Wilde on playing "Bea" in **Paradise Lost** (2006).

So here we are then. A global economy with travel seemingly accessible to all, a convergence of cultures, a meeting of minds a….well, well hang on there just one minute. The world may well seem a smaller place, we may appear to be closer in physical if not emotional proximity to our cousins across the earth, but perhaps all this has achieved is to highlight our cultural, religious and social differences, to heighten the tensions between us, bringing into sharp focus the divided planet we inhabit.

For this particular filmic travel brochure reveals not so much a glorious surf of optimism riding a wave of cultural enlightenment but rather a stagnant tributary of positively Stygian proportions, meandering its way inexorably towards a bloodied and confused coda. In the minds of a certain brand of modern filmmakers we check-in to see not a passport to paradise but a one way trip to Hades.

Paradise Lost

Just as Adam is warned by Raphael not to eat the fruit of the Tree of Knowledge in John Milton's *Paradise Lost* – "And govern well thy appetite, lest Sin surprise thee, and her black attendant Death", so too the protagonists of Roth's **Hostel** series and their insatiable appetite for free sex and cheap drugs discover that their "vices" will inevitably bring about their own death and destruction.

For Paxton (Jay Fernandez), Josh (Derek Richardson) and Oli (Eythor Gudjonsson), their backpacking trip from the red light district of Amsterdam to the "flesh dens" of Bratislava in Slovakia, becomes an ordeal more appropriate to a "last breath or "last minute(s). com holiday booking if you will.

The trio, with their prurient palettes satiated with the promise of a hostel "to die for" (literally as it transpires), awash with gorgeous babes just waiting to spread their favours (and themselves) for American guys – like, right?!

Embarking on their own form of "Gullibles Travels" via train, they encounter a cryptic Dutch businessman (Jan Vlasak) whom Paxton casually berates for eating his salad lunch using only his hands – "I prefer to use my hands. I believe people have lost their relationship with food. They do not think "this is something that died for me so that I would not go hungry." I like that connection with something you die for. I appreciate it more."

Paxton's response that "Well, I'm a vegetarian" is countered with "I am a meat-eater. It is human nature." Paxton's reply that "Well I'm human and it's not in my nature" elicits an uneasy tactile response as the businessman's coded enquiry; "Tell me... what is your nature?" is delivered whilst also placing his hand on Josh's leg – understandably freaking him out as the stranger then makes a hurried, apologetic exit.

This is a pivotal scene in Roth's film. When the three friends later do discover their imagined babe-laden hostel, their night of unconditional coupling with their sexy roommates prove to be not quite as "free" after all as they find themselves awake in a cavernous, underground torture chamber, with the furtive businessman reappearing as one of their chief tormentors.

Hostel 2

Hostel 2

His need to "touch" his "prey" and to "connect" lends a chilling emphasis to his previous statement. Although the bloodbath that Roth promised upon the release of **Hostel** never truly materialises, the violence here being gruesome but purely perfunctory, it's the films myriad of themes which inspire further interest.

     The power of money is inverted here with some irony as Josh, tied to a chair and rendered helpless in the torture chamber, begs the Dutchman; "Please! I have money. I'll fucking pay you. Ten times, whatever you want!" "Pay me?" is the puzzled reply. "No one is paying me. In fact, I'm the one paying THEM!" (referring to the shady Elite Hunting – an underground organisation where members pay for the "privilege" of torturing and killing the "caught to order" victims – a kind of "ebay" with bodies).

     Likewise, when Paxton realises he has been duped by the vivacious Natalya (Barbara Nedeljakova) and left imprisoned in the charnel house lair, he accuses "You fucking whore. You fucking bitch!" "I get a lot of money for you and that makes you my bitch." This ironic reply to Paxton indicates that it is he who is now at the bottom of the food chain – the axis shifting from the opening scenes where the backpackers are the "moneyed" tourists, able to buy who and what they please in the red light district and yet the carnal pleasures of that hedonistic haven are now a distant memory having been replaced by the cruel pain of the torture chamber.

Their previous display of arrogance and cultural xenophobia returns to haunt them as their "Grand Inquisitor" is now the Dutchman who is both economically and authoritatively their superior now. The role reversal is completed by the film going against the grain by also having the guys and not the girls suffering from their drinks being spiked – this is not date rape but death row however.

Paxton's previously crass comments "I hope bestiality is legal in Amsterdam, because that girl's a fuckin' hog" and christening the Dutchman on the train as "Edward Saladhands", resonate with a hollow echo now. His (unwitting) entrance into the torture chamber is even accompanied with the cautionary quip that "You could spend all your money…in there." Of course, the dual currencies on offer here are money and human life – Paxton may posses both but only one fatal currency will be accepted

Hostel 2

Hostel 2

from him now.

Leaving aside the rather bland, time-consuming opening where plastic discos and a distinct lack of character development reside – what Roth succeeds most at is in conveying a real sense of helplessness and inevitability to the proceedings. Although Josh, Oli and Paxton are all rendered as merely one-dimensional characters, almost ciphers for the prejudices that their attitudes simply confirm, the moral choices which confront Paxton towards the denouement serve to up the ante and engage the viewer.

He is the only "victim" who manages to make good his escape – a genuinely tense sequence as he is secreted amongst a trolley of bloodied body parts – rising through the Dante-like levels of horror within the torture complex, before eventually reaching the freedom that the fresh air above will herald.

Being so close to escape and yet perhaps in a futile attempt at redemption he returns to the underground dread in order to save the now mutilated figure of a fellow hostage Kana (Jennifer Lim). Given that when he releases her from her torment – her one eyeball now residing precariously on her cheek, she implores him to cut it off, to which he reluctantly obliges

Hostel 2

her – a squirm-inducing scene which is far more effective than Roth's rather lame torture scenes which precede it.

Having completed their daring escape Kana then supplies a thoroughly bleak and valedictory moment by preferring to leap to her death in front of a speeding train rather than take her chances living in such a brutal and brutalising world devoid of hope.

Roth's well documented genesis for **Hostel** – having stumbled across a website where you pay for the opportunity to kill people for "thrills" indicates just how desensitised we are now post 9/11, where executions can be watched/downloaded for free in the name of Jihad. As Roth reveals, "Real or not, there are people so numb to their own existence they are looking for the ultimate high. Porn isn't enough anymore, but killing is – and that's too terrifying to contemplate." One of the American clients, a would-be torturer even indulges in some callous "locker room" banter with (a disguised) Paxton – "I've been all over the world. You know, I've been everywhere and the bottom line is pussy is pussy. You know, every strip club, every whorehouse, every…it's all the same shit. You know I just fucked a girl two days ago and I don't even remember the colour of her tits. But this…this is something you never forget, right?"

Whereas the captivity aspect inherent in **Hostel** also alludes to the current world conflicts as well as informing the **Saw** film series, together with such luminaries as **Captivity** (2007) and **Vacation** (2007), it is the culture conflicts which most permeate the film. Given the colliding realities of the insular American psyche against (though not exclusively) the Muslim world and indeed much of Europe's mistrust of both American ideologies together with American military and economic power. It is crucially observed in **Hostel** that the ubiquitous Elite Hunting members will pay more for US victims than for any other nationality – merely reflecting you could argue the wider, prevailing world view.

For Roth however, the charge remains that he is having his cake and eating it – by attempting to portray American stereotypes to then condemn them one could argue that he is simply serving to reinforce them. Besides the outdated view of women there is also the small matter of Slovakia being portrayed almost "Borat" style as an underdeveloped, crime-ridden

Hostel 2

Hostel 2

backwater, rife with prostitution and unseemly ghettos and yet for all the "Eastern Europe" pontificating here, we are basically describing a middle-European city not unlike the more fashionable cities Roth's characters relate to. It has to be said though that in Roth's defence, Slovakia's record on human rights regarding ethnic minority groups isn't the most unblemished within EEC circles.

Given that the protagonists headlong descent into their doom in **Hostel** and the incidental plot frailties – kids street gangs paid in gum to help kill the captors pursuing Paxton and Kana through the streets anyone? - the characters remain lacking in the detail of say the backpackers equally terrorised in the Australian outback in Greg McLean's engrossing **Wolf Creek** (2006).

There's also the small matter of the final plot contrivance where the now fleeing Paxton just so happens to discover that the eponymous Dutchman is also travelling on the same train. The final moments as Paxton corners him before dispatching him in a toilet cubicle provides a cathartic end to the violence (for now at least) - a sense of deep satisfaction and

rough justice meted out but is a contrived rather than a credible conclusion to events.

With the inevitable follow up **Hostel 2**, Roth succeeds in adding some further nuances to pique the interest but you can't help feeling that the sound of tills jangling (given the huge commercial success of the original) has led to Roth somewhat compromising artistry on the altar of commercialism.

Plot-wise it's a case of as you were with the same Slovakian setting and three protagonists unwittingly awaiting slaughter in the torture chamber. The main departure this time however, is we have three girls rather than guys lined up for the trials of a gruelling Elite Hunting experience. The luxury of hot spring spas rather than the basic frugality of a hostel lends a pampering element to this experience compared to the original film.

The stereotypical characters here include the rather sluttish tough girl, Whitney (Bijou Phillips), Lorna (Heather Matarazzo), the rather nerdy, almost too sweet torture-fodder and finally, Beth (Lauren German) the rich, confident, sassy girl with lesbian tendencies. Seduced by a statuesque model Axelle (Vera Jordanova), the girls are inveigled into the torture chamber having been drugged as per the original film.

Once again there is little in the way of real surprise – just "gorno" as the gore/porn phrase is coined, or "**Hostel** plus a B cup" as one wag noted. "This is bullshit" spits out one victim with "No, this is business" being the stark riposte – perhaps emphasising the avarice over content ethos of what will no doubt go on to become a film franchise?

Roth's main attempts at character development revolve around the would-be executioners from Elite Hunting – Todd (Richard Burgi) and Stuart (Roger Bart) with the human auctions aspect made explicit rather than implicit here as we see the miscreants bidding online for the "right" to torture and kill the female victims.

Within the dynamics of their relationships we see Todd as the typical sporty type, whilst Stuart is the more introverted family man with some homoerotic tendencies. Besides a purely perfunctory submissive/dominant dichotomy in their relationship, further development here is eschewed rather than investigating the potentially intriguing interplay between the hunter and the hunted.

Although the film has been pilloried for misogynistic traits, the films as a whole provoke a compelling moral debate as to what is the most insidious – the slaughter of horny guys in **Hostel** or the violating of vivacious girls in **Hostel 2**? It's a similar moral quandary alluded to in the one truly chilling moment in **Hostel 2** when the Elite Hunting alumni Sasha (Milan Knazko) learns of deception from one of his own who is operating outside of the auspices of the Elite group – shooting him off screen and therefore in bloodless fashion, contrasting vividly with the all too bloody demise afforded to the female protagonists.

The Dante's "inferno" of the former film is complimented here (if that's the right word!) by the Nietzschian notion of gazing long into the abyss – "oh, how they spiral down into even deeper depths" as the protagonists embark upon their inevitable path with more than a hint of Greek Tragedy.

Whilst Roth undoubtedly hits some major concerns in his **Hostel** entries, there remains the nagging suspicion that he somehow fails to realise the full potential of such an intriguing and provoking premise – given further credence in the hostile milieu of the world today.

His wit and intelligence is nowhere as sharp as the torture

Paradise Lost

Paradise Lost

instruments which pervade his films, albeit blunted by his Tarantino-like self indulgence (see **Death Proof** (2007)!) and his somewhat slavishly fan boy insistence on talking the talk as regards blood, gore and flesh, yet singularly failing to deliver on any real sign of suspense, subtlety or insight to elevate his work. As *The Village Voice* bemoaned of his ethos in **Hostel** as being somewhere between "frat boy porno wish fulfilment" and a "Europhobic sex tourism scare flick."

Just as the world isn't their oyster but seemingly their eventual prison for Roth's protagonists, it remains to be seen whether he can build upon the early promise of **Cabin Fever** (2002) with his future work, including the adaptation of Stephen King's *Cell*.

One could also argue that it has taken Roth three hours to do what Koldo Serra's little seen gem, **El Tren de la Bruja** (2003), did in 15 minutes . With more tension, more scares, it captures the true horror of a man, in the dark, tied to a chair whilst taking part in an obscure experiment. He hears metallic objects being handled accompanied by the sound of someone pacing about the room – ultimately, he realises he is going to be tortured to

Paradise Lost

death when suddenly the light is turned on.

Although not descended directly from **Hostel**, John Stockwell's **Paradise Lost** (2006) explores similar themes to Roth's oeuvre but jettisons his "smorgasbord of sex and drugs in Europe" in favour of a more overtly exotic, South American locale, Brazil.

Once again, there appears to be a kind of cultural xenophobia at work here as a cosmopolitan group of tourists from the "civilised" world find themselves at the sharp end of some local "hospitality" in the unforgiving rainforests of the relatively "uncivilised" Brazil. When their coach party is stranded on a mountainous road, Alex (Josh Duhamel), his sister Bea (Olivia Wilde) and her friend Amy (Beau Garrett), along with others in their party, make their way through the nearby woods to the "promised land" – in this case a golden beach, waves lapping the shore and music playing in the nearby bar to complete a picture of idyllic paradise.

Having hooked up with the roguish local Kiko (Angles Steib) they party on the beach well into the night. When they awake the next morning with the mother of all hangovers it's a case of "Bom Dia, Cinderela) or

"Good Morning, Cinderella" as the aptly-named drug means they will not go to the ball as they no longer posses either money or passports – all taken from them during the night in their haze-filled stupor.

With Kiko coming to the "rescue" it's a case of "with friends like this…" as he leads them through the jungle to his uncle's remote cabin and away from the angry villagers they have upset on the way.

Unfortunately, all they find is savagery rather than salvation in the form of the sanguinary Zamora (Miguel Lunardi) who it transpires is running a lucrative black market in human organs with the steady stream of foreign tourists being the unwilling donors. "Did you know in America there is a seven year wait for a healthy kidney" he proudly announces, scalpel poised ready to slice up yet another unfortunate victim, in his best "Dr. Butcher" fashion a la **Zombie Holocaust** (1980). As critic Philip French would have it Zamora does indeed "make Dr. Moreau look like Dr. Kildare" justifying his misanthropic approach on the grounds of third world revenge against first world imperialism.

Charged with raping his land of rubber, sugar, gold, and using its

Paradise Lost

Severance

people as sexual playthings in the many forms of sex tourism perpetrated against them, Zamora wreaks his revenge against this exploitation by plundering the vital organs from these transgressors. "I'm doing this for a good cause." His bedside manner definitely requires some work one feels, continuing in similar vein; "I'd take the heart and even the skin from their lilly white asses if I could…but they don't travel well."

By selling the organs for the almighty dollar Zamora can't exactly claim the moral high ground, even if he claims to be emancipating his countries finances with the proceeds – "The whole history of our country is you taking from us" he admonishes, claiming a justification by claiming; "What does a Gringo do if he gets sick? Does he wait on a donor visit? Or does he come to a third world country like ours and buy organs from one of our children? I'm only balancing this out."

So whilst the surgical imperative in **Hostel** is purely based on the individuals lust for the thrills and inflicting pain, in **Paradise Lost** there is a more powerful raison d'etre, albeit as equally misguided as in Roth's films.

Ironically, the "business" in body parts which Zamora has embarked upon is just the prosaic, mundane transaction the Dutch surgeon/torturer in **Hostel** so readily eschews in his keynote speech – "I always wanted to be a surgeon. But the boards would not pass me. Can you guess why? You see? (hands shaking) So I went into business. But business is so boring. You buy things, you sell them. You make money, you spend money. What kind of life is that? A surgeon, he holds the very essence of life in his hands – your life. He touches it. He has a relationship with it. He is part of it."

Despite Stockwell's attempts to put flesh on the bones of Zamora's character (with the reverse true of Zamora's victims), he remains an under developed character, with the plot as under dressed as the beach-clad bikini babes who proliferate at the film's start.

Much akin to Roth, this cosmopolitan group of characters including Brits, Americans, Swedes and Australians, are still a sketchily drawn band who it is difficult to have any real empathy for. As Finn (Desmond Askew) exclaims at one point; "I hate this. I don't like it at all. I like beaches and drinking and girls. In all the ads they say come to Brazil. We've got

Severance

Severance

beaches and drinking and girls. They don't say we've got vicious, angry mobs that chase you into the jungle."

Hence, the characters stereotypical, purely superficial concerns are brought to the fore ready to be ridiculed, equally in their slavish following of Kiko for over ten hours through the jungle – a figure they hardly know or can trust which stretches credibility somewhat.

Likewise as in the **Hostel** series, there is minimum suspense – the most effective sequence being the suitably claustrophobic underwater chase sequence as Bea is forced to out swim Zamora's henchmen, periodically surfacing to gasp for air from miniscule pockets above the surface in the underground cave system. Only some poor lighting dissipates the inherent tension here as well as during the closing stages when the group escape the cabin operating theatre amidst the night rain lashing down to compound the gloom.

As with the **Hostel** films Stockwell's film concludes with a kind of cathartic violence where the "hunted" hit back to become the "hunters" – their initial hopes of sun, sand and sex in an exotic environment, by now

Severance

trailing and forgotten in their wake. To simply survive the ordeal is victory enough now.

Whilst the **Hostel** series and **Paradise Lost** delineate a particular brand of backpacking tourists as both a thematic device and as plot advancement, Christopher Smith's spirited **Severance** (2006) replaces the tourism motif with a workplace and teambuilding riff instead.

Smith, whose previous outing **Creep** (2004) saw a lone German girl stranded overnight in the London underground (a scary enough thought on its own!) along with all manner of rapists, drug users and cannibals for company, centres the action in **Severance** in an equally inhospitable location (as it transpires), set in woods on the Hungarian/ Romanian border.

Mixed moral messages are readily apparent as employees from the Palisade Defence company – a multi-national weapons outfit, are left stranded in a derelict building after their coach breaks down, with no obvious means of communication in the remote forest, only to be attacked by a coterie of crazed killers.

Aside from the obvious morality questions of working for a company selling arms and thereby perpetuating warfare in the world, the ensemble cast are forced to fight for their very lives against the maniacs who are wielding guns, knives and flamethrowers as well as utilising land mines and bear traps to inflict the maximum injury possible.

Thus, we are introduced to the requisite number of office stereotypes including; the plebby Gordon (Andy Nyman), the foxy lady Maggie (Laura Harris), the sweet but dull Billy (Babou Ceesay), the haughty graduate Harris (Toby Stephens), the cheeky chappie Steve (Danny Dyer) and the office bore Jill (Claudie Blakley), all presided over by the vacuous Richard (Tim McInnerny) – "I can't spell success without u" being his cringe-inducing mantra – soundly repelled by Harris' terse "There's only one 'u' in success."

Described as being anything from "*The Office* meets **Deliverance**" to **Ten Little Indians** (1965), **Severance** demonstrates a vicious strain of black humour to good effect and differentiating it from the previous films discussed here, and yet this is also perhaps the films "Achilles heel" as

Severance

Severance

the dynamics of merging the survival aspects with the politics and foibles of a typical office, ditto work environment are sometimes lost amidst the jokes.

The besieged group struggling to survive in a hostile, alien environment against a voracious enemy betrays the **Dog Soldiers** (2002) and **Wilderness** (2006) influences, requires the feisty Maggie and ebullient Steve to cut through the corporate posturing typified in Richard's naive indoctrination, talking of Palisade that "It's a public company. Members of both our governments are on the board. They're not going to do anything immoral", the sentence almost crashing down under the weight of the irony. It is just this kind of corporate duplicity which endangers the group in the first place and is responsible for the numerous casualties – Steve, the lone male survivor, along with Maggie and the nubile Olga (Juli Drajko) and Nadia (Judit Viktor) – "foursome" being his hopeful rather than expectant final words!

Given that many of these filmmakers are 1970's kids – growing up during the post-Vietnam period on gritty, uncomfortable horrors such as

Severance

The Texas Chain Saw Massacre (1974), **The Hills Have Eyes** (1977) et al where cinema offered a release or escape from the pent-up angst of the nation, it is clearly where this new breed of equally disquieting films has erupted from in our post 9/11 society.

The so-called "splat-pack" including such luminaries as Roth, Rob Zombie and Alexis Aja are simply responding to the prevailing tensions of social, political and religious instability worldwide. As Greg McLean succinctly observes upon the contemporary horror film and his own success with **Wolf Creek** – "The reason people responded so well is because it's irrefutably horrors job to take us to the edge of what's acceptable in society. It allows us to jump across the abyss, open the curtains to the other side, then scurry back quickly into the light of day. The closer you are to the terrifying edge, the more alive you feel. Isn't that what you sign up for when you choose to watch horror?" A compelling summation with which to end.

The Thing: America and the Fight Against Communism.

Matthew Edwards

Science Fiction film has fascinated and fuelled the public's imagination, especially, in the respect of the progression of science and the widespread myth of stories of "aliens from Mars". Inspired by such texts as H.G. Wells *War of the Worlds* and Mary Shelley's *Frankenstein*, a whole generation of movies sprang up based on such theories. When probing beneath the surface, Science Fiction films, in general, are considered as more than mere B-movies, for they become recognisable as a product of their time, highlighting fears and dangers relevant to their culture at that particular point. Science Fiction films, most notably during the 40's, 50's and 60's, can be seen as a basin for the expression of political views and opinions that were not easily harvested in mainstream pictures. Any politicising was strictly forbidden, suppressed. Significantly, both cinematic versions of **The Thing** show us two very different Americas in relation to the threat of Communism. Howard Hawke's version is considered as an anti Communist propaganda film, calling for the need for containment in light of the developing cold war. Truman's fear of the enemy within was explicitly stressed, as well as the need to rally together in order to nullify the spread of the Marxist disease.

In Carpenter's version, the specific emphasis focuses on America's involvement in Vietnam, at once condemning, whilst playing on the motifs of isolation, division, de-humanisation, that would consequently bring forward notions questioning who the enemy really is. Ultimately, what is presented before us is two startlingly different America's when confronted against the Communist threat. One shows us a united America, elated from their success in World War II and their global supremacy, ready to stamp out any threat or movement that does not comply with their way of thinking. The other America paints a totally different picture; one that showed its people radically split and in conflict over an issue that was considered as no concern of the US. A nation ultimately divided.

Both film versions of **The Thing** were based on the novella *Who*

Goes There? by John W. Campbell writing under the pseudonym of Don A. Stuart. Set in an isolated research station in the Antarctic, the group discovers the remains of a creature trapped in ice. In respect to both films, Carpenter's version is more faithful, playing upon the idea of the alien masquerading as one of them, employing the themes of distrust and paranoia, especially evident to the experiences and feelings of those soldiers who fought in Vietnam.

Who Goes There? was originally filmed as **The Thing From Another World** in 1951. Released by RKO films, it can be justifiably seen as one of the best monster movies to emerge from the giddy heyday of Sci-Fi/horror film fodder. The film is typical of those during this era with the lead characters constant bantering and the lack of coherent logic. Although not a bad thing, it seems making cups of tea or playing cards on your own is perhaps not the most constructive thing to be doing when there's a rampaging alien on the loose.

The Thing from Another World was unlike other similar movies of this period that would lend its support to the allied decision to drop the A-bomb. Many movies of this ilk were quick to capitalise on the new atomic age and the development of higher calibre weapons. A real interest had been generated with the dropping of A-bombs on both Hiroshima and Nagasaki, so a new guile of weaponry was introduced to stun and fascinate American audiences, dwelling on their supremacy. Although these advances in weaponry were reserved for the aliens, minds boggled as to whether America could duplicate such weapons. **The Thing from Another World** in contrast lacks any ray guns, strange costumes, or futuristic inventions, with the spaceship only suggested at.

At the time there was overwhelming support for dropping the Atomic bomb, at once ending Total War and saving the lives of millions of Allied and American soldiers. Some movies like **The Day the Earth Stood Still** (1951), did begin to question the bomb's usage, and carried a simple underlining message that we must care about humanity and our planet, instead of destroying it, especially as the long-term effects and consequences of radiation exposure to both the people of Japan and American servicemen became more apparent. In **The Thing from Another World**, one character comments "we split the atom and that sure made the world happy". Although disguised with laughter from members of the cast, this brings forward a cynical view in terms of using nuclear bombs against humanity. Distrust for science parades throughout the film, epitomised with the character Carrington whose scientific methods become more and more scrutinised. The need to exercise control and develop safer means for nuclear energy became a prevalent idea, and one that was the most logic and rational.

Hawke's version definitely shows us an America in a period of transition, a whole nation basking in their global dominance, justifiably proud of their military might. It certainly shows us a united America, whom would rally together and support one another. This reflects in the obvious subtext of the movie: the need to tackle and stamp out the threat of Communism, which plagued the minds of politicians, most notably Truman.

Science Fiction films were the perfect guise for subliminal subtexts, as they could be woven into the overall fabrication of the story. Using clever metaphors, some cinemagoers were oblivious to such messages, at the same time giving writers the opportunity to put forward fears producers felt awkward dealing with head on.

The threat of Communism spreading is very much in evidence when analysing **The Thing from Another World**. During this period America saw the need for containment in respect to this dangerous ideology, and what it propagated and was attempting to implement. Russia was trying to assume global control with Marxism, at once threatening Western cultures and American interests. In the 1951 version of **The Thing** it is essential for the Americans to stop the Thing from spreading, taking over the world.

This relates to the US, where the fear that Communism was spreading, and gaining support, became one of Truman's principle concerns. Russia had been an American ally during the Second World War, however Truman held nothing but contempt towards Stalin and viewed him as a potential enemy. Any hope that the wartime alliance would carry over into post-war proved to be nothing but another great illusion. The early signs were clear, for trouble arose when Russia began setting up compliant governments in Eastern Europe, violating the Yalta promises of democratic elections. Considering the Allies had just stopped the threat of Fascism, the chance of Communism breaking out throughout Japan was something the American's could ill afford to ignore or tolerate.

This alien ideology sabotaged the American belief of democracy, so Hawkes played on this heavily. The prime example, and most frequently

used, was the alien was an allegory of a Communist. What they, and their alien crafts, represented was the outside threat becoming the enemy within. They believed they could brainwash the masses into joining their so-called perfect ideal. The alien would therefore be only solely interested in world dominance. It sent out the message that anyone could become corrupted into joining the Marxist cause. As brilliantly detailed in **Invasion of the Body Snatchers** (1956) and the Science Fiction classic **Invaders from Mars** (1953), anyone could wake up a Communist, a brainwashed zombie. This fear that can be traced back as far as the pro Communist rallies in New York in the 1920's.

Hawkes depicts the Thing as a huge bloodthirsty super humanoid that lacks emotion, morals and, is ruthless in pursing his one objective, to poison and take over the human race. The creature looks human in every respect, except a couple of characteristics. Perhaps, this is where the horror lies. He looks so human, suggesting anyone could harvest Marxist tendencies, as well as anyone could sympathise with them.

This provokes similarities with the McCarthy witch-hunts, which surfaced in 1950. Revelations about State Department infested with Communists saw Joseph R. McCarthy begin a crusade, claiming he held a list of names of those in office whom sided with Marxism. McCarthy simply exploited the situation and general Communist hysteria. In fact, he never actually uncovered a single Communist agent in government. Although McCarthy was playing on the public's fear, the whole debacle simply showed that paranoia was sweeping across the US like a plague. American was turning against American, and it does suggest how fearful the threat from within had become.

Therefore containment was essential. **In The Thing from Another World**, the creature is trapped inside a block of ice; it had been contained and suppressed. When it escapes it posed the threat to civilisation. Rallying together, Captain Hendry and his men devise a plan to exterminate the Thing, and prevent it from contaminating mankind. This rallying is echoed with the news of China's embracing of Communism, after America failed to side together coalition governments. This was a big blow to America, for they had viewed that with a newly united and reinvigorated China they could play a key stabilising role. This shocked America who had for a long time held great affections towards China, and they had assumed they were nurturing them under their tutelage towards Christianity and democracy.

The Thing

To America, the loss of China was regarded as almost parricidal.

This sparked off the Korean War, where again we see parallels to Hawke's version, as we see Hendry's men attempting to re-capture their government station, as the Thing terrorises the premises. It therefore can be considered as an allegory of the Korean War and America's strategy to contain and break up Communism. A detailed study of the Korean crisis reveals significant evidence showing the Soviet's intentions, of applying Marx's sociological doctrines to whip up support and to cause a proletarian revolution, consequently demolishing the old class system, leaving a new era of social justice that sees the political authority of the state dying out.

The filmmakers were propagating this motive that Communist ideologies had increased to an alarming level, therefore as respectable thinking human beings, we must confront these evils, eradicating them at once.

With Hawke's version, the idea that the Thing resembles a plant symbolises the belief of Communism sowing their crop seeds, nurturing and then reaping the harvest when their ideologies had been successfully implemented. This brings forward the view that Communism was embedding their roots, making a shift away from Marxism very difficult.

When the Thing re-grows his arm it suggests a never-ending battle to stop Communism, however uniting together against this foe, you can at least contain it. As Truman once said, "one rotten apple would infect the entire barrel".

Out of all the characters, the Scientist Carrington seems the most suspicious, envious and fascinated by this creature he describes as "wiser and more intelligent". In his laboratory, Carrington conducts experiments, before realising it contains no animal tissue, just green fluid, therefore, not human. He likens the Thing as a vegetable, or, "a super carrot". He states to the group that it experiences no pain or pleasure, no emotion, no heart, before declaring the Thing as "so superior".

Carrington has become sucked into the false belief that we can learn from these creatures. "If only we could communicate with it". It is obvious by now that Carrington has been corrupted into secretly admiring the Thing, continuing experiments where it lives on blood. Carrington consequently grows his own batch of the Things. This reinforces the idea of spreading their seeds, Carrington here being their vital link. Carrington is unknowingly manifesting his own little army, that will in time overthrow and conquer. Michael Weldon comments, in the *Psychotronic Film Guide*, "the plant creature uses human blood to nurture its seeds, and some scientists at the base help them grow. The more sensible military leader puts a stop to that nonsense".

Carrington has fallen into the Communist trap, firstly attracted, then helping, before finally being disposed of when the creature has no more value with him. It is then up to Captain Hendry and his men to stop the threat of the alien, saving civilisation. With echoes of Roswell and the hysteria brought around the supposed crashing of an alien ship in 1947, we are urged to watch the skies. Or is that for Commies?

In contrast, John Carpenters **The Thing** (1982) shows us, unlike Hawkes version of a united America, but one still reeling over America's involvement in the Vietnam War. **The Thing**, perhaps one of the greatest modern horror/Sci-Fi films superbly details how paranoid and distrustful they had become against each other. America's participation in Vietnam saw condemnation at home from its own people, as millions of young Americans protested to conscription, at once dividing the nation.

From the out start America's involvement was questioned, even more so when American genocide was brought to the forefront, most notably with the My Lai massacre in 1967. Suspected of being a NLF stronghold, American soldiers systematically murdered a total of five hundred unarmed civilians, raped the women and girls, pillaged, butchered their animals and used babies and small children for target practice. It was news stories like these, upon there return to America, that society viewed them as outcasts and not trustworthy. It was this isolation question and human emotion that Carpenter played heavily upon in the remake of **The Thing**.

The fact that **The Thing** is set in the Antarctica only serves to highlight the isolation of our protagonists. They are in a foreign land. This relates back to Vietnam, where the value of human spirit battling against insurmountable odds in a hostile environment was very much in evidence. Having fought in this foreign land, they returned home to somewhere equally as foreign and alien. They had become isolated from their own society, outcasts, which relates directly with MacReady, a Vietnam Vet and helicopter pilot, whom is simply escaping his troubles back home to make some quick bucks. MacReady himself reinforces his isolation. As Anne Billson comments, in the *BFI Modern Classics* book on **The Thing**, "he's a bit of a loner, playing computer chess, rather than something more

The Thing

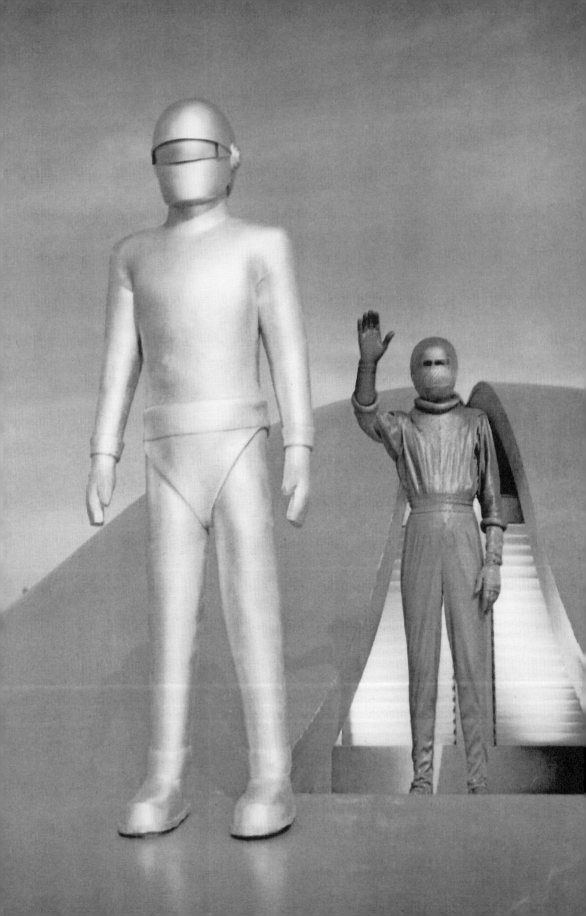

sociable as Ping-Pong".

Carpenter plays further with the isolation question. When Blair goes crazy, smashing up helicopters and the radio equipment, it brings forward the notion that "if the men were isolated before, now there's absolutely no way that any of them can escape".

This inevitably leads to paranoia, as the characters begin experiencing every negative human emotion, from despair to terror, amid scenes of pointless bloodshed and violence. This creates a divide, a harrowing eroding of their souls. It's as if Carpenter's holding up a mirror, reflecting images back of Vietnam.

The conflict between Carpenter's characters relates directly to America's experience in "Nam". There is constant bickering over status that eventually causes a split in the unit, a common trait that surfaced in the platoons that fought in Vietnam. Often members would take sides, and this echoes to that of Childs and MacReady, whom fight for leadership of the group. Their distrust for one another is evident, each believing the other to be the Thing. At times the group is too busy fighting themselves instead of

The Day The Earth Stood Still

uniting together to defeat the enemy. This re-enforces the split back home in America, a dilemma spiralling out of control.

A key example of this is exemplified during the blood serum test, with the men shown as isolated and vulnerable. There is clear distrust towards each other, not helped by the items of shredded clothing. "Nobody trusts anyone now"; mutters a tired MacReady earlier in the film, summing up the over-riding feeling of suspicion and divide. With the players tired to chairs, fear and paranoia has finally overcome them.

This relates to Vietnam in the sense brother was against brother, or, American against American. As Charlie Sheen so aptly describes in Platoon, "we did not fight the enemy, we fought ourselves, and the enemy was in us". This perfectly sums up the situation.

Carpenter using the parable of the alien within us, morally showed and brought home that America's defeat in Vietnam was self-inflicted. With the idea of the alien masquerading as one of them, their downfall came from the political will of the government, as the anti-war movement grew, a less positive outcome loomed as the war dragged on, and the casualties rose.

America's sole intent on crushing Communism in Vietnam sees parallels inside the film with MacReady declaring, "we're not getting out of here alive, neither is that Thing". Does this suggest America would have been prepared to destroy itself and its reputation to ensure that Communism could not spread? It is significant to point out that America was willing to sacrifice public opinion, when stopping Communism polluting throughout Asia. This was compounded even more so during the Tet offensive in 1968 that ultimately snapped the spirit of Lyndon Johnson, who decided not to run for election in 1968.

Another factor you could label similarities with Carpenter's version and the experiences of Vietnam troops was that they never really knew who the enemy was. Although they were fighting on the side of the Southern Vietnamese, they often complained they were fighting the wrong side, with the South Vietnamese not fully appreciating what they were there to do. Carpenter played on this factor, resorting back to Campbell's version when using the Thing as a shape shifter, an impostor whom imitates other life forms taking on their guise. The enemy therefore could be any one of them. For example, apart from MacReady we assume Blair is the only character also human. We are led to believe that by destroying the

helicopters and radio communications he is trying to contain the alien, stop it spreading. When we learn that Blair has been infected, you wonder has the Thing been incubating in him all along, and importantly is it Blair's shadow we see earlier with the husky dog? This is an important factor, as Carpenter played on the idea of keeping the viewer guessing whom the enemy in the midsts was. A theory echoed again back to those whom fought in Vietnam.

Other theories connected to experience of Vietnam and **The Thing**, was the American Marine Core's de-humanisation of its troops. Under their rigours training regime, the recruits were slowly turned into capital robots, designed simply as killing machines.As Matthew Modine would comment in Stanley Kubrick's **Full Metal Jacket** (1987): "if you scrape the veneer a little bit and get into man's psyche, he becomes an animal". He states also that the boot camp isn't about characters or personality, just the sole intent into turning soldiers into killers. In an interview with Caryn James of the New York Times, Modine would comment, "You're taught your whole life not to hurt other people, not to kill other people; but when you go into a system like the Marines, those rules suddenly don't apply anymore".

How this reflects onto Carpenters version is that his characters are very real, undergoing every emotion possible. However, when they become infected they become de-humanised, a replica no longer human. **The Thing** hits them where it hurts, undermining their sense of individualism. The Marine Core was creating theses replicas, by which their only instincts were to kill. Anne Billson puts forward the idea, "is that man next to me and inhuman monster?" These people, consequently, are no longer human, perfectly summed up with the ginger hared Bennings who is transformed into the Thing. He is now no longer the man he used to be, supporting the idea of them becoming de-humanised. When they have succumbed to being the Thing, their only intention is to contaminate the collected group. They are simply killing machines, devoid of any emotion.

The underground bunker where Blair has built an aircraft is very similar to the Vietcong bunkers in Vietnam. These long thin tunnels act as a labyrinth, where Carpenters characters are forced to endure and nullify the threat below. The same can be applied to those in Vietnam who had to adventure within the underground tunnel system, taking out snipers and the Vietcong in general. MacReady has to destroy the bunker if he is to eradicate the threat from spreading. There is also a case to suggest the sniper threat, which dominantly was a primal factor when sweeping through an abandoned Vietcong village. In one instance during **The Thing**, Blair is acting like a sniper, as the rest of the group cowers, shielding for cover. They seem to resemble a platoon caught in the line of fire. This was one of the common fears Marines had to experience in Vietnam. They would have to be on their guard all the time.

Both film versions of **The Thing** show us how culturally different America had become. The threat of Communism needed to be controlled, but where as the Howard Hawkes' version portrays America as united and proud of their world status, John Carpenter's **The Thing** presented an America less interested in interference into foreign politics unconnected with theirs. Many felt there were to many problems at home to worry about, without adding Vietnam as another one. This attitude may have been a reason for the subsequent Isolationist Foreign policy the US adopted, until the events of September 11th, and subsequent attack on Iraq, that saw them engage more in global issues. It highlighted a split in their society, at once alienating the participants on their return. John Carpenters **The Thing** is as mad as the war was itself, with the characters as confused and distrustful as the marines that fought.

Hawke shared Truman's philosophy. Their fear of loss of identity, particularly the individual's fear of being swallowed by a faceless mass was very much in evidence, and can be considered an allegory of the totalitarian political system. By the end of his picture his players have successfully united to defeat the common enemy, saving at once mankind.

When examining John Carpenter's version, the downbeat ending gives off a defeatist attitude, suggesting they may not have contained the Thing. Ironically, it is MacReady and Child's who are the principle survivors, sharing a few suspicious words, no longer caring. Child's absence leads you to suspect he may have become one of them, supported by the fact MacReady breath is revealed as icy cold, yet any traces of Child's icy breath are not forthcoming. Maybe, like America in Vietnam, they failed ultimately to stop the threat of their common foe.

Marshall Law

Andy Black

In 1999 the then fledgling UK director Neil Marshall directed an early short film **Combat** delineating the battle between the sexes, given a heightened sense of irony as the sound of warfare replaced any dialogue – an ambitious riff on an age old subject and perhaps the perfect training ground for the conflicts to come in his later work.

The particular conflicts in question are introduced in **Dog Soldiers** (2002) and its filmic alter ego **The Descent** (2005). Although both films are ensemble pieces, portraying groups in extreme danger, Marshall's ingenuity is in reaffirming the human spirit in **Dog Soldiers** whilst simultaneously dismantling it in **The Descent**. Both films benefit from Marshall's insistence on building characters, offering up realistic motivations as well as being able to satisfy even the most jaded gore hound with his bravura scenes of action and carnage.

Marshall makes the precious distinction in **Dog Soldiers** that "I set out to make a soldier movie with werewolves, not a werewolf movie with soldiers" - the basic premise here pitting army squaddies on a training mission in the Scottish highlands against a legion of seven feet tall werewolves intent on decimating all in their path. A kind of "Saving Private Ryan with werewolves" if you will as has been noted by some critics as it is the genuine camaraderie between the soldiers which elevates **Dog Soldiers** above the average, yet at the same time being humorous, exciting and scary in equal turns.

With Marshall's follow up **The Descent**, this sense of camaraderie remains superficially, but in reality the group of all female cavers soon descend themselves into internal bickering as their situation in becoming stranded by a rock fall beneath the bowels of the cave system they are exploring brings all manner of tensions to the surface that their physical bodies so desperately crave.

As Marshall reveals; "I always wanted to do a horror film set in a cave…you can't get any more dark than this" as our primal fear of the dark is exposed to devastating effect.

It's not so much a fear of the dark but what's in the dark which

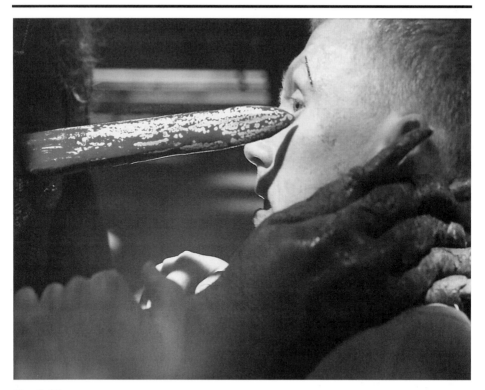

Dog Soldiers

propels **Dog Soldiers** as Sergeant Wells (Sean Pertwee) and his second in command, Private Cooper (Kevin McKidd) as they lead their troop on exercises in the remote woodland, only for their "training" to be abruptly curtailed upon the discovery of the slaughtered remains of a Special Operations Squad. Only their commanding officer Captain Ryan (Liam Cunningham) survives (his earlier encounter with Cooper revealing how he failed Cooper's attempt to join "Special Ops" for refusing to shoot a dog as ordered) – "I need men of action, not deeds" he admonishes the soldier. So, instantly our sympathies here lie with the "humane" Cooper rather than the officious, calculating Ryan.

Amidst a backdrop of dripping blood in the now destroyed camp, the eerie howling in the peripheral distance is the precursor to the cogent scenes of the squaddies running literally for their lives from the (as yet) unseen assailants – merely towering silhouettes within the shadows of the darkening woods.

Forced to seek refuge in a nearby farmhouse the beleaguered soldiers are then besieged by their lycanthropic invaders as they are now revealed. The force's subsequent defence of their impromptu base, together with their ultimately doomed attempts to flee in the jeep parked outside, instantly pay homage to similar scenes in George Romero's **Night of the Living Dead** (1968).

Despite the claustrophobic confines of their barricaded location there's a real "espirit de corps" here as tensions may rise but their support for one another is unwavering, despite the repeated werewolf onslaught they are required to repel.

Their outlet valve for releasing tension is the black humour which lies ingrained in their approach to the situation. This is none better illustrated than in the gallows humour inherent as the wounded Wells suffers the indignity of seeing his "sausages" (intestines to you and me!) being frantically pulled at by an excited dog – unravelling them like a line of the aforementioned meat. "My guts are out Coop!" Wells shouts in pain – "Well, just put them back in then" being Cooper's abrupt reply. "They're not gonna' fucking fit" Wells cries back hilariously (to us) – "Of course they'll fit man" counters an unsympathetic Cooper. Cue comical scenes

Dog Soldiers

Dog Soldiers

later as they try to stuff his intestines back inside by using that well known medical aid – superglue!!

"Ever wondered why the best thing that superglue sticks together is your fingers? Forget your grandma's china cups – this stuff was developed for the Vietnam war to patch up broken soldiers" explains Cooper to a sceptical audience. Asked how he's feeling, Wells pithy reply is "A touch of gas. And the fact that various body parts are trying to vacate the premises, fucking awful!"

The troops are regaled earlier by Wells fabulous "camp-fire" story which perfectly skirts the tightrope between dark humour and a sense of real foreboding, narrating the tale of one Eddie Oswald, a squaddie whose "Faustian" pact with the devil results in him being blown up during the Iraq conflict. His body parts are scattered to all four corners of the battle theatre save for his legendary arse tattoo proudly proclaiming that "Satan saved his skin." As Wells explains; "So you could say that Eddie was right. Satan did indeed save his skin, just not all of it. Or you could say that Eddie was just unlucky. Either way, it taught me to keep a very open

mind. Boom boom." It's an open mind they will all need to comprehend the werewolf mayhem surrounding them now.

Despite the confined area of the farmhouse, Marshall's roving camera exhibits an almost expansive space as each room of the building is explored and utilised by the end of the film. It is this duality which also underlines the pivotal quandary as to whether they should flee their base – does it offer security or will it ultimately become their prison? It is safer to take your chances outside amongst the baying werewolves or is it safer to stay inside utilising the protection afforded by the four walls of the farmhouse.

As the tensions heighten the camaraderie in **Dog Soldiers**, so they begin to unravel the intrinsic character frailties in **The Descent**. On the anniversary of a white water rafting trip which ends in tragedy as her husband and daughter die in a car accident, Sarah (Shauna MacDonald) embarks on a new adventure potholing in the Appalachian Mountains of North Carolina, along with self-appointed leader Juno (Natalie Jackson Mendoza), English teacher Beth (Alex Reid), feisty punk Holly (Nora-

The Descent

The Descent

Jane Noone), climbing expert Rebecca (Saskia Mulder) and her half-sister Sam (Myanna Buring).

As Saskia Mulder explains on her role as Rebecca – "You can see the fracturing of friendships and the fracturing of minds." It is not so much a fissure as a gaping chasm that ends up eventually separating Juno from Sarah – the formers trenchant attitude serving only to attempt to prove herself to be the ace caver, rather than supporting her supposed friend Sarah in order to help restore her shattered confidence and self-belief in the wake of her bereavements.

Juno's self-serving conceit only succeeds in endangering the entire group as she jettisons the guidebook in favour of secretly pursuing a new, unchartered cave system which they subsequently become trapped within.

As Juno sheepishly admits of the cave in the aftermath of the rock collapse to her "chicks with picks" ensemble – "It hasn't got a name. It's a new system. No one's ever been down here before. I wanted to discover it." "So, this isn't caving. This is an ego trip" Rebecca spits back at her candidly.

Marshall expertly galvanises his "terror tools" in order to embellish the film with a compelling urgency and a genuine sense of claustrophobia. As the girls narrowly squeeze themselves through the network of labyrinth passageways there is the constant sound of water trickling, permeating the mind like an elaborate Chinese water torture, harnesses clank, boots echo, bodies slide against the gravel, human breathing is amplified to unsettling proportions in the dank tunnels. Only the fading glow of the cavers helmet lights, together with the sporadic crimson and vermillion flares illuminate the dark intensity with an almost ethereal glare.

Sarah's understandable panic attack as she tries vainly to crawl through an impossibly narrow passage invites the lame response of "What are you afraid of? The worst thing that could happen to you has already happened!" A false prophecy if ever there was one as the palpable sense of claustrophobia and isolation that Marshall has cultivated in the film's first half with its real life physical traumas then dovetails, into the Grand Guignol of a frenetic second half as the cavers realise that they are not

The Descent

The Descent

alone… They discover that they must not only fight themselves but also the grotesque, cannibalistic "crawlers" who inhabit the caves – an unwelcome atavistic addition to the cave fauna.

The almost Gollum like crawlers evoke the subterranean cannibals of **Death Line** (1972)and **Creep** (2004), and as if the iconic imagery of cramped tunnels and ghastly personal injury (Holly falls down into a stony pit leaving her bone protruding awkwardly from her bloodied knee), aren't gruelling enough, the presence of the crawlers adds to the prevailing sense of despair and nihilism in what has now become an endurance test for sheer survival.

Betraying some human characteristics and appearance traits the crawlers offer a primordial take which is reinforced by the ancient cave drawings the cavers discover earlier on their journey, as well as the rusting caving equipment they stumble across – evidence that the group are not the first to attempt to navigate these caves or indeed the first would be victims – a theory authenticated by the eventual disclosure that they are surrounded by hundreds of skeletal remains.

The creatures first appearance – eerily lit by the glare of a flashlight to lend a spectral air to the sequence, is expertly handled by Marshall and he discussed the exact timing of this in painstaking detail with his crew in order to wring the maximum suspense and impact from the moment.

In much the same way, the werewolves from **Dog Soldiers** are given a similarly staged entrance for optimum effect – distant howls, shadowy outlines to begin with until their glistening teeth and velvet claws are illuminated by the omnipotent moonlight. They too offer a primal threat – a decidedly hirsute but non the less believable extrapolation from the human frame with the traditional silver bullet replaced by a silver letter opener here as the preferred method of dispatch.

One of the most intriguing aspects of both **Dog Soldiers** and **The Descent** however, is the machismo which we find expectedly present in the former film but unexpectedly in the latter. In **Dog Soldiers** the male ensemble exhibit an entirely naturalistic display of macho posturing – the need for thrills, for action and indeed thriving on danger almost. With the all female ensemble in **The Descent**, there is a certain irony in finding the

The Descent

same macho traits within many of the cavers as their infighting leads them into becoming as savage as the unforgiving milieu they now inhabit.

The dichotomy of the female characters tends to veer between macho heroines or female screamers, with certain members being physically strong but morally weak, especially when confronted with the choice of being either buried alive or gorged upon by cannibals. Perhaps this can also be glimpsed as a sly observation on the "ladette" culture where women can behave as badly as men without fear of peer reprisals.

Just as the guys in **Dog Soldiers** enjoy their barracks humour, whether it be dissing Special Ops', talking about girls or the football – "We are now up against hostile targets. So, if Little Red Riding Hood should show up with a bazooka and a bad attitude – I expect you to chin the bitch", so do the girls engage in some locker room banter; Beth jokes to Sarah as she lies trapped in a tunnel – How do you give a lemon an orgasm? Tickle its citrus!" (Marshall did however cut some "Carry On" style dialogue at the female cast members' request so there is no "squeezing through tight, wet cracks" left to alleviate the horror).

The Descent

The Descent

Interestingly, the solitary female character in **Dog Soldiers**, Megan (Emma Cleasby), a local zoologist, appears initially to be the sexy counterbalance to all that uncontrolled male testosterone. The subsequent reveal that she is indeed one of the werewolves herself, lends added intrigue to the proceedings as if she acts as a kind of portal for the creatures – "They were always here. I just unlocked the door" she confides regarding the lycanthropes. Even her own eventual transmogrification is given a peculiarly feminine twist – "Let nature take its course…it's that time of the month." As she continues her philosophy – "I came here to be at one with nature, well I got what I wanted. Now I have to live with it." Megan concludes cryptically that "Up until today you believed there was a line between myth and reality. Maybe a very fine line sometimes but at least there was a line. These things out there are real. If they're real what else is real? You know what lies in the shadows now. You may never get another nights sleep as long as you live."

In order to reinforce this nightmarish image Megan confirms to Cooper that "You may think all women are bitches…but I'm the real thing."

As if to continue this lineage in **The Descent**, the particularly intense personal rivalries between Juno, Sarah and Beth propel the pernicious plot dynamics into new areas of "bitchdom". As Beth pleads in vain at one point during the film; "I'm an English teacher, not fucking *Tomb Raider*."

Sarah, haunted by recurring visions of her dead daughter, perhaps is prepared to take on the mantle of *Tomb Raider* by jostling with Juno as their descent into the interior of the gloomy cave dwellings acts as a metaphor for their own spiralling descent into madness.

Where Marshall really scores in spades here is in assembling a group who are not merely the stereotypical slasher-fodder of horror film convention but a feisty, tooled up coterie kitted out for the fray. Whilst the carefully crafted character studies are slightly nullified by the frantic finale, it still delivers the ideal platform for Sarah to rise to the fore – bloodied by her encounters with the crawlers, she becomes indistinguishable from the crimson-coated abattoir she now inhabits – at one point propelled into a cess pool of human remains a la Dario Argento's **Phenomena** (1987). Hampered by the haunting presence of her daughter, Sarah blames Juno

The Descent

entirely for their hopeless plight and exacts her supreme revenge by taking an axe to Juno's leg and leaving her bleeding and immobile as the amassed hordes of crawlers menacingly begin to encircle her. Juno's anguished screams resonate through the caves as Sarah is making good her own escape.

There's a particularly potent ending as we see Sarah's outstretched hand punctuate the outside world as she hauls herself from out of the gloom and scrambles up into the bright sunlight. An overwhelming sense of euphoria and exhilaration is felt now that she is "free". A deliberately ambiguous coda leaves both a lingering doubt as to whether Juno has also managed to survive, but also hazards a guess as to Sarah's own mental state as the camera tracks slowly away, isolating Sarah and her child as if in a still life tableau – perforated by the chilling screams of the ubiquitous crawlers.

As a riff on the dangers of ill-advised adventure tourism, **The Descent** can be seen as a cautionary tale but it also nods equally to the Freudian "womb anxiety" motif, symbolised by the organic nature of the network of tunnels, the taut sense of claustrophobia and the much heralded "rebirth" conclusion as Sarah reappears into the outside world.

By utilising the dynamics of group concerns and fears, rivalries and frailties, Marshall has fashioned an extraordinarily thought provoking duo of films, one the flipside of the other, both inexorably linked stylistically, emotionally and thematically as if by some latent umbilical cord. As James Christopher wrote in *The Times* of **The Descent**, "The gore leaves nothing to the imagination and everything to your next nightmare."

With the inevitable sequels planned – **Dog Soldiers : Fresh Meat** (2008) and **The Descent 2** (2009) it will be fascinating to see how Marshall also fairs with his next opus, **Doomsday** (2007) – set in a post apocalyptic future where a military team in an "infected" zone cut off by a thirty feet high wall, search for a cure to the "Reaper Virus".

If anyone can scale the heights to find it, one would imagine that Marshall can.

Quatermass and Carpenter

Steve Earles

The influence of Nigel Kneale's Quatermass films, particularly Hammer's 1967 production of **Quatermass and The Pit**, runs deep in the work of John Carpenter. This is particularly evident in **Prince of Darkness** (1987) and **Ghosts of Mars** (2001).

At the time of the release of his now classic **Escape from New York** (1981), Carpenter said, 'Those Quatermass movies of yours are some of my favorite movies of all time, you know. I love them. I love Nigel Kneale." (Though he probably doesn't love him now.) "I understand **Quatermass and The Pit** was probably the best."

Hammers Anthony Nelson Keys asked Roy Ward Baker to direct the cinema adaptation of **Quatermass and The Pit**, the third of Nigel Kneale's Quatermass stories.

Baker was a distinguished director, most famous for **A Night To Remember** (1958), and he would go on to direct a number of classic Hammer films such as **Dr. Jekyll and Sister Hyde** (1971) and **The Legend of the 7 Golden Vampires** (1974). Baker was as impressed then as John Carpenter would be, he said of **Quatermass And The Pit** in his autobiography: "It was taut, exciting and an intriguing story with an excellent narrative drive. It needed no work at all. All one had to do was cast it and shoot it."

But the history of **Quatermass And The Pit** began almost ten years earlier as a six part BBC television series, broadcast in live thirty-five minute episodes between December 1958 and January 1959. It was watched by one in three British viewers. Two years later, Hammer Film Productions optioned the screenplay and planned to remake it as *The Pit*, to follow its previous Quatermass films, **The Quatermass Experiment** (1955) and **Quatermass II** (1957).

Unfortunately it proved difficult to raise co-finance in the US and it would be another three years before the final draft of Kneale's screenplay, now titled **Quatermass And The Pit**, was delivered, and two more before the film went into production.

Kneale retained most of the essential elements from the series,

In the Mouth of Madness

though the location was moved from a housing development at Hobb's Lane to a central line extension at the Hobb's End underground station (In John Carpenters Lovecraftian tale **In the Mouth of Madness** (1994), the town Sutter Cane writes in is named Hobb's End in honour of Kneale.)

Baker cast James Donald as Dr Mathew Roney. Julian Glover played Colonel Breen, the officer put in charge of the excavation. Duncan Lamont, who had played Caroon in the BBC version of *The Quatermass Experiment*, was cast as Sladden. Hammer favorite Barbara Shelley would play Barbara Judd.

Quatermass himself had already been played by several actors. Reginald Tate in the BBC's *The Quatermass Experiment*, John Robinson in the BBC's *Quatermass II*, Andre Morell in the BBC's *Quatermass And The Pit* and finally Brian Donlevy in Hammers previous *Quatermass* films.

Kneale didn't like Donlevy, and was assured a replacement would be found. Andrew Keir was to become the fifth actor to play Quatermass. His performance was best summed up by Roy Ward Baker – "Andrew

Keir was certainly the best of the Quatermasses and was acknowledged by all and sundry."

Elstree studios was too busy to accommodate the film, so MGM's studios at Borehamwood were used instead. The finished film was released in the UK in November. In the US the film was released under the title **Five Million Years to Earth**.

Hammer's film of **Quatermass and The Pit** remains faithful to the key elements of the BBC serial, with workmen uncovering human remains estimated by paleontologists to be around five million years old. An excavation also finds what they initially believed to be an unexploded V-rocket from the second world war, but when Professor Bernard Quatermass investigates, he begins to suspect the 'missile' is a spacecraft made by beings who have assisted mankind's evolution to their own ends. His theories are quickly proved to tbe terribly true. Keir gives us a wonderful Quatermass, passionate in his pursuit of the truth, with scant regard for his won reputation (a proto - Mulder, if you will). His antithesis is Julian Glover's Breen, typically military, rigid and unbending. He doesn't see the

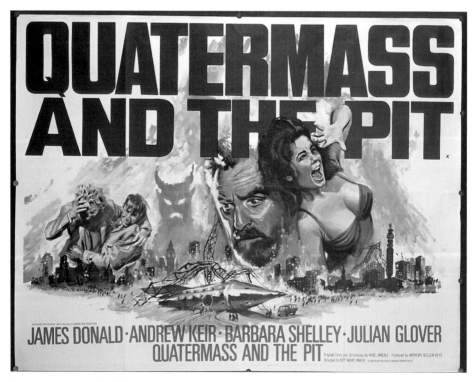

Quatermass and the Pit

truth until it carbonises him.

Quatermass And The Pit can stand proudly as a Hammer classic alongside such films as **Plague of the Zombies** (1966) and **The Devil Rides Out** (1968). More importantly, it's a highly influential film, with strong scripting and intriguing ideas such as the influence of extra terrestrial intelligence on mankind's evolution and a synthesis of the occult and science with the paranormal phenomena caused by the buried aliens, attributed to demons. Quatermass is hugely influential on TV series such as *Doctor Who* and films such as **The Astronauts Wife** (1999) and **Lifeforce** (1985). It influenced many who went on to create films, not least of all John Carpenter.

Carpenter has always acknowledged Kneales influence. Having fallen out with Kneale over **Halloween III: Season of the Witch** (1982), Carpenter would go on to pay homage to him in 1987 with **Prince of Darkness.**

Prince of Darkness followed bigger-budgeted studio films such as **The Thing** (1982), **Christine** (1983), **Starman** (1984) and **Big Trouble in Little China** (1986). The studio interference on **Big Trouble in Little China** was the final straw, so Carpenter decided to sacrifice big budgets in return for greater creative control.

Prince of Darkness was the first film of a four-picture deal with independent company Alive Films. The four films were to be low budget and delivered within a five-year period. With worldwide presales, each one would be in profit before their release. Sadly, only one other film, **They Live** (1988), was produced.

While Carpenter wrote **Prince of Darkness**, the credits for the film list the writer as Martin Quatermass. The press book for the film includes a biography for him – "Martin Quatermass, born in London, England, is a former physicist and brother of Bernard Quatermass, the rocket scientist who headed the British Rocket Group during the 1950's. Quatermass graduated from Kneale University with a degree in Theoretical Physics. Prince of Darkness is his first screenplay, and he assures that all the physical principles used in the story, including the ability of subatomic particles to travel backwards in time, are true. Author of two novels, *Schrodingers Revenge* and *Schwarzwald Radius*, he currently lives in Frazier Park, California, with his wife Janet."

At the time of the release of **Prince Of Darkness**, Carpenter said

– "I've been a fan of Nigel Kneale's work for years and years and this was a homage to show how much I admired him. Dedicating the script the way I did was the best way I could communicate this to him. His work means a host of different things to me on a number of levels."

"I was a big fan of the Brian Donlevy Hammer movies when I was a kid because they had a mix of ideas from science-fiction and H.P. Lovecraft all thrown together and I had always been attracted to that. When I went to London in 1977, I got my hands on the three BBC scripts which had just been published in book form. Reading them I realised his talent for writing dialogue coupled with the descriptive passages all had the ability to chill. I think his style as a writer and his power are unique. I had the opportunity to work with him briefly on **Halloween III: Season Of the Witch**, which I co-produced, but at that point Nigel was very embittered about the way of the world as was shown I think in *The Quatermass Conclusion*. That was the only unfortunate part of the experience and I specifically remember Joe Dante and I trying to convince him that **Quatermass II** was a brilliant movie while he thought it was awful. The fact that he owned the rights and literally withdrew the movie from circulation was due to him thinking it was bad. We were begging him not to even consider it."

Sadly Kneale's feelings for Carpenter weren't mutual. "Each time you say to yourself, "if they make this one it will be my best" and very often it will be the one that doesn't get made or it will get so drastically changed you take your name off it. A few years ago I wrote for John Carpenter and we fell out simply because I'd produced what I thought was a very nice script which was chopped down budget wise and reduced in every way, so I took my name off it. It was **Halloween III**. The premise of it was that it would owe nothing to either **Halloween** (1978) or **Halloween II** (1981), except for a glance at the title. It was to be a totally original story, different from anything he'd made. Interestingly enough, one day he said, "I wish I'd directed **Quatermass II**" which I wish he had in some ways. In other ways I don't know – he might have done something terrible with it."

Carpenter did extensive research on quantum physics in **Prince of Darkness**. The film mixes quantum physics with religion, questioning the nature of what we perceive to be reality. The parallel with **Quatermass and the Pit** is obvious, with Satan (interestingly, one of the nicknames given to the World War II V Weapons was 'Satan') long entombed in the crypt of a

Quatermass and the Pit

downtown Los Angeles church (named Saint Goddards, another Carpenter homage), on the verge of being released from a millennia old canister that can only be opened from the inside. Donald Pleasance's character confronts the ultimate betrayal. Christianity has characterized evil as dwelling in the hearts of mankind, now his world is turned upside down as he discovers evil exists outside of man, and the Church has always known this. **Prince of Darkness** is also a siege movie in the spirit of Carpenters hero Howard Hawks.

Both films hide the answers to their questions in ancient books. Both films feature foreboding warnings of the evil to come. In **Prince of Darkness**, ants and worms swarm in unnatural fashion, as Satan's power increases he begins to control the street people and move objects to influence events (the unfortunate woman who becomes the vessel for Satan receives a bruise in the shape of an alchemic symbol that Carpenter got off a *Blue Oyster Cult* album). In **Quatermass and The Pit**, as the machine in the pit's influence grows, people literally become Martians, reliving memories of hive-cleansings. In **Prince Of Darkness** the messages come, not from the past, a distant race memory, but from the future. Anyone in close proximity to the cylinder in the church crypt shares the same dream, a warning sent from the future. Both films feature ancient evil, entombed for millennia, being awoken to extend an influence on the humans above. After all, Hell is traditionally below ("I saw a star fall from Heaven unto the bottomless pit").

In **Prince of Darkness**, the evil literally enters its' host, in **Quatermass and The Pit** it is already there. Carpenter skillfully employs the same synthesis of sorcery and science as Kneale in **Prince of Darkness**. Satan uses the scientist's own computers to tell them neither faith nor technology will save them – " You will not be saved by the Holy Ghost. You will not be saved by the god Plutonium. In fact, YOU WILL NOT BE SAVED." (A later message is all Carpenter's when a zombie held together by swarming insects tells his former friends to "PRAY FOR DEATH".)

Ghosts of Mars uses one of the central ideas of **Quatermass and The Pit**, that of Martian possession. Set in a future where mankind is terraforming Mars, a scientist inadvertently releases the spirits of a long dead Martian race. The spirits find suitable human hosts and mutilate them in imitation of their previous form. In the same manner as the hive-cleansings seen in **Quatermass And The Pit** on the 'optical encephalograph' machine developed by Dr Roney to observe suppressed racial memories of a Mars populated by insectiod aliens. This is achieved in **Ghosts of Mars** by Natasha Henstridges character Melanie Ballard having a flashback to the original Martians under the influence of a drug. Kneales idea of a buried evil, not just beneath the ground, but within us, is best summed up in **Quatermass and The Pit** by Quatermass himself. One being told by a priest who has tried to help the possessed Sladden – "I felt sure he'd been in contact with spiritual evil." Quatermass surmises – "perhaps it was always in him. In all of us."

The appreciation of Kneale's influence on Carpenter is as important as element of understanding Carpenter's work as that of the influence of Leone, Lovecraft and Hawks.

Neo Zombies –

Repression, Rage and Resurrection!

Andy Black

"In fact, we philosophers and 'free spirits' feel ourselves irradiated as by a new dawn by the report that the 'old God" is dead'; our hearts overflow with gratitude, astonishment, presentiment and expectation. At last, the horizon seems open once more, granting even that it is not bright; our ships can at last put out to sea in face of every danger; every hazard is again permitted to the discerner; the sea, again lies open before us; perhaps never before did such an 'open sea' exist." **Friedrich Nietzsche**

"Don't blame the mirror if your face is a mess." **Nicolai Gogol** in *The Government Inspector*

Perhaps the 'new dawn' and the 'open sea' which bookend Zach Snyder's 'reimagined' **Dawn of the Dead** (2004) remake weren't exactly what Nietzsche had in mind but the 'life-affirming drive' demonstrated in the recent zombie film renaissance would have perhaps led to Nietzsche allowing himself a wry smile.

As with any film genre some of the entries vary wildly in quality and substance with peripheral titles such as Uwe Boll's **House of the Dead** (2003) Mike Hurst's **House of the Dead 2** (2005), Michael Bartlett and Kevin Gates **The Zombie Diaries** (2006) and Scott Thomas' **Flight of the Living Dead** (2007) riding in the slipstream of a number of pre-eminent titles which I plan to discuss here. Also, not to forget Robert Rodriguez' high profile pulp flick, **Planet Terror** (2007) – a return to the cheesy seventies 'grindhouse' style complete with babes on bikes, limb lopping and oodles of gore. In addition to Snyder's energetic **Dawn of the Dead**, the maestro, George A. Romero himself has been busy completing the fourth instalment in his zombie mythology with **Land of the Dead** (2005), as well as the forthcoming **Diary of the Dead** (2007) – already so lauded that a further entry in the cycle has been green lighted.

Together with the **Resident Evil** series – Paul W.S. Anderson's

Planet Terror

Resident Evil (2002), Alexander Witt's **Resident Evil:Apocalypse** (2004) and Russell Mulcahy's **Resident Evil:Extinction** (2007), plus Danny Boyle's **28 Days Later** (2002) with John Carlos Fresnadillo's sequel **28 Week Later** (2007), this zombie film rebirth provides a fascinating commentary on modern times by returning, ironically, to one of the classic staples of the horror creature pantheon. As Nietzsche himself would have it – "He who fights with monsters should look to it that he himself does not become a monster."

These neo-zombies do flirt with the prevailing post 9/11 milieu with Dennis Hopper's turn as the manipulative, self-serving oligarch Kaufman in **Land of the Dead** being based upon the (then) US Defence Secretary Donald Rumsfeld. "We do not negotiate with terrorists" he even utters at one point and in another shot a plane that has crashed through a building can be clearly seen. In **28 Weeks Later** a now quarantined London is presided over by US military forces in an echo of the Iraq conflict – "The US army is responsible for your safety" being the mantra perpetuated here. Fears of mass immigration are also relegated to a secondary status

– scenes of amassed zombies attacking cities almost as if an 'alien' race apart feature prominently in **Land of the Dead**, **Dawn of the Dead** and especially in **Resident Evil:Apocalypse**.

For some of the most absorbing themes however, we need to return to Nietzsche's philosophy on the dystopian society we now find where social and structural disintegration prevails, morality and religion all but disappeared. For Nietzsche the nihilism which is written large across the atrophying 'civilisation' is not the end point but the beginning – just what will replace the old order? In this decaying world current conceptions of value are rendered bankrupt, quite literally so given that money itself is now an outdated currency with no meaningful value at all.

Indeed in **28 Days Later**, **Dawn of the Dead** and **Land of the Dead** we see repeated scenes of the protagonists raiding shops and malls for food, drink and medicine – money is no longer the prerequisite to ensure survival but rather it is the armoury provided by a hand gun or rifle that has supplanted it. This is no better illustrated than when the aggrieved Cholo (John Leguizamo) attempts to blackmail the unrepentant Kaufman

Planet Terror

Land of the Dead

for the sum of five million dollars. The size of the sum is in effect rendered pointless as it begs the question – where will you go and what will you do with all this money?

The reason for Cholo's antipathy towards Kaufman is firmly rooted in his aspirational attempts to escape the 'slave' or 'working class'mentality/morality of the masses inside the walled city, in favour of the pseudo-aristocracy or 'master class' living the high life (literally) in the skyscraper monument to social and economic avarice – the Fiddler's Green complex. Vacuous tv ads play on a continual loop extolling the sanitised 'virtues' of living in this (ironically) glass-filled environment. Why the need to advertise when we are informed by Kaufman that the elite block is now fully occupied anyway and just how do the inhabitants reconcile their wealth and luxury in contrast to the unfortunates scraping an existence out on the streets below, perilously close to the army of zombies roaming the outer walls of the city? It also raises the spectre of the First world's attitude to both the starving and the refugee population in the Third world.

It is also slightly incongruous that Kaufman maintains his position

of authority seemingly by the use of financial power when it is simply physical force which now obtains goods and services. As the embittered Cholo – now infected from a zombie bite, utters the film's best line; "I always wanted to see how the other half lives", ouch!

Kaufman's subsequent demise – callously shooting a so-called colleague before exiting to the underground car park, laden with suitcases full of (worthless) money as if clinging to the last vestige of the 'old order' and its values, is deeply symbolic. So too is his selfish attitude and scorn shown towards the black chauffeur – quite clearly seen by Kaufman's vile ogre as being subservient to him. The copious amounts of cash and fuel in his revving car ultimately count for nothing as he is set on fire in an ugly demise.

Romero has always been one of the most class conscious of his film peers and in addition to Kaufman's rich, white Republican (most surely) and Cholo's downtrodden, undervalued Mexican, **Land of the Dead** is populated with some rather sterile characters.

From Riley (Simon Baker), a kind of old-fashioned working class

Land of the Dead

Land of the Dead

hero just seeking to survive and escape the city in the ubiquitous 'Dead Reckoning' armoured vehicle – "I'm looking for a world where there are no fences" he announces at one stage, more in hope than expectation. A momentary lapse into idealism totally out of kilter from the seemingly hopeless situation he finds himself in. As realism sets in again the prospect of seeing the zombies 'pretending to be alive' provokes the icy response of; "Isn't that what we're doing? Pretending to be alive?" He also remarks at one point that "I'm fed up with back stories", a charge sometimes laid at Romero's for concentrating on the political rather than the emotional values of his characters. Whilst Asia Argento's Slack is rendered as the rather perfunctory 'hooker with a heart (and gun!) and Charlie (Robert Joy), as the loyal sidekick to Riley, it becomes clear as always with Romero that his true sympathies lie not with the humans but with the zombies.

The impression is forged that we should identify more with their egalitarian world – or at least it is in comparison with the social injustice ingrained within the human city. Big Daddy (Eugene Clark) continues the traces of humanity and intelligence instigated with Bub in **Day of the Dead** (1985). Whilst the 'civilised' content themselves with hanging zombie corpses upside down to shoot at for target practice or throw them 'gladitorial' style into contests where Slack is offered up as 'bait', Big Daddy leads the undead march onto the besiged city.

In **Land of the Dead**'s most celebrated sequence, he is the first one to dare to jump into the river, surviving to lead the silent army as they emerge en masse from the dark, mist-laden water, bathed eerily in the moonlight and now ready to advance upon the now looming (and unsuspecting) city populace. (This also serves as Romero's own *homage* to one of his favourite films, Herk Harvey's **Carnival of Souls** (1962) where the dead materialise from Great Salt Lake).

This sequence is also noteworthy as it presents us with a literal manifestation of Freud's dictum concerning the 'Return of the Repressed' which expounds the notion of dreadful truths returning to haunt the human psyche like nightmares. Just as a vampire is repelled by garlic so to are the zombies expected to be repulsed by water, but by crossing this physical (and psychological?) boundary the nightmare is made real. As Charlie remarks pointedly at one stage; "I have bad dreams. Hell, yes. Just look at

Land of the Dead

Dawn of the Dead

me, you can tell I have terrible dreams."

This 'nightmare' of not only advancing zombies but 'intelligent' zombies is also reinforced during the climax as Big Daddy stands, omnipotent in the entrance to the underground car park in calculating repose as he calmly rolls a firebomb down the trail of leaking petrol to ignite Kaufman in his car.

Only a somewhat frenetic pace which ushers in the finale detracts from an otherwise effective, if flawed return to the zombie genre for Romero – his 'updating' of the mythos only extending so far without fully realising the potential for a more contemporaneous take on the subject – he does manage one ironic concession to reflect modern trends however, by filming the first zombie bite on a stomach piercing with one unfortunate victim!

Zach Snyder's **Dawn of the Dead** displays no such wanton scenes of 'metal wear', not even a 'piercing' critique of consumerism as with Romero's original **Dawn of the Dead** (1978), preferring instead to concentrate on greater action and considerably faster zombies as with

Danny Boyle's **28 Days Later**.

The opening scenes depict a convincing collapse of the social infrastructure as emergency tv broadcasts urgently warn about the 'plague' enveloping America. There's an incredible aerial shot – not of the expected urban sprawl but the leafy suburbs, the very heartland of the American Dream now shown to be rapidly engulfed in flames and chaos. Everywhere people are running, shooting indiscriminately at anyone they suspect to be zombies as cars crash, homes burn and people die, all perforated with the incessant tv broadcasts now indicating this to be a global epidemic.

Whereas Romero's original film delineates two groups of survivors fighting each other as well as the omnipresent zombies, to offer a further dynamic, Snyder reverts to pitting the human ensemble against the attacking zombies but as Snyder has dispensed with the consumerism satire as well the mall setting becomes almost incidental and our sympathies again turn towards the zombies who cannot be held responsible for their behaviour whereas the humans most definitely can, and thereby reducing the impact of any inherent 'good versus evil' axis.

Dawn of the Dead

Dawn of the Dead

Snyder's new clique of survivors are in fact shown to have a diverse range of motives and personalities, embodying the Nietzschian concept of 'immorality' – where a good person can be a 'creator of values' as morality is dictated by human nature but this nature is not universal. One individual's nature is different to the next so people follow differing conceptions. The dying value systems depicted so convincingly in the opening anarchy, render there to be no virtue in obeying God so the fictitious promise of greater rewards in the next life cannot be used as an excuse for the subjugation of the spirit in this one any longer. The 'superman' or 'ubermensch' premise of Nietzsche rejects this in favour of carving out one's own place in the world.

As an original **Dawn of the Dead** survivor, Ken Foree's cameo here as a tv evangelist allows him to signal civilisations decline and also reprise his iconic lines from Romero's opus; "Hell is overflowing, and Satan is sending his damned to us. Why? God is punishing us. You have sex out of wedlock. You kill your unborn. You have man on man relations, same sex marriages. How do you think your God will judge you? Well, friends,

now we know. When there's no more room in Hell, the dead will walk the earth." Glen (R.D. Reid), who we learn played the organ in church delivers his own doctrine; "It was just a job...I don't believe in God. I don't see how anyone could."

Those waiting to be judged, or perhaps aspiring to their own new ideals – 'the lightning out of the dark cloud of man' as Nietzsche would have us believe, include; Michael (Jake Webber) who is a shrewd, intelligent protagonist who deviates between recalling a life before zombies to being shown as having the ruthless streak necessary to survive. Ana (Sarah Polley) a nurse, who is bright and composed rather than just the obligatory female screamer and Kenneth (Ving Rhames), an ex-marine now gun-toting cop who becomes the group's de facto leader.

Kenneth also supplies some of the film's bleak humour by communicating with Andy (Bruce Bohne), a gun store owner across the mall, who transmits messages by using a dry wipe board from the top of his roof. He also plays 'sniper' in shooting at the 'celebrity look alike' zombies below – "Tell him to shoot Burt Reynolds!"

In amongst this eclectic mix we are also introduced to Andre (Mekhi Phifer), a reforming street hustler whose hopes of redemption lie with his pregnant girlfriend Luda (Inna Korobkina) – ultimately proving to be false hopes with the subsequent birth of their 'zombie' baby in a well executed scene.

Completing, or should that be 'competing' with the survivors are the triumvirate of security guards CJ (Michael Kelly), Terry (Kevin Zegers) and Bart (Michael Barry) – CJ offering the couch potato outlook on humanity, detached from the collapse of the society he vicariously experiences via the banks of monitors he gazes into in a numbing display on desensitivity. This trio, especially in the form of the selfish CJ, would prefer to keep the mall to themselves rather than risk letting in other survivors – the nearest Snyder comes to evoking the human conflict intrinsic to the original.

It is the sheer size of this ensemble, to almost soap opera proportions, which merely succeeds in dissipating the tension of the situation as there are simply too many characters on which to focus, diluting any personal interplay and dynamics. The racial divide so prevalent in **Night of the Living Dead** (1968) evolves here into a strictly class or cultural divide with both Kenneth and Andre as mixed race Americans, generating the most tension within the group and its fractious, continually expanding

Resident Evil

factions.

The complete lack of governmental presence, indeed of any authority figures or response in both **Land of the Dead** and **Dawn of the Dead**, is a factor perhaps unexpectedly addressed in the **Resident Evil** trilogy. While it is perhaps too much to hope for any enduring substance or perceptive insight to emanate from, what after all, is a film series based on a video game series, there are some intriguing aspects of corporate experimentation and manipulation permeating the series which also acts as a metaphor for the absence of any Machiavellian government being in place.

True, the entire series does rest hugely on the more than capable frame of the gun-wielding, high kicking, action figure of Alice (Milla Jovovich) who truly does embody Nietzsche's 'ubermensch' philosophy – in **Resident Evil:Apocalypse**, her partial infection by the 'T-virus' leads to her development of 'superhuman' strength, as well as showing telekinetic powers in **Resident Evil: Extinction** as she levitates both giant rocks and an off road bike to dramatic effect.

It is the ubiquitous Umbrella Corporation, which, as the name implies now threatens to envelop the entire USA with its nefarious, experimental research, DNA cloning and related technologies. As the narrator in **Resident Evil** obligingly details; "At the beginning of the twenty first century, the Umbrella Corporation has become the largest commercial entity in the USA. Nine out of every ten homes contains its products. Its political and financial influence is felt everywhere. In public, it is the world's leading supplier of computer technology, medical products and healthcare. Unknown, even to its employees, its massive profits are generated by military technology, genetic experimentation and viral weaponry."

It is the genetic cloning aspect of the Umbrella Corporation's work (truly a shady company in both name and deeds), which unleashes the aforementioned 'T-virus' in their underground facility 'The Hive' – conveniently explained to us by the computer generated hologram the 'Red Queen' as being 'protean, changing from liquid to airborne to blood transmission, depending on its environment. It is almost impossible to kill,'

Resident Evil

Resident Evil:Apocalypse

continuing ominously that 'Just one bite, one scratch from these creatures is sufficient. And then you become one of them.'

It is instantly noticeable how the Umbrella Corporation reacts immediately upon the accidental release of the virus – summarily gassing their employees in order to contain the virus but also the inevitable bad publicity and ensuing corporate share meltdown which is the implicit message here.

Ironically, as Romero was originally slated to direct the film, his influence is never doubted as Alice, resplendent in miniskirt and boots, aided by Matt (Eric Mabius) and an elite force (of course!) including Rain (Michelle Rodriguez), then proceed to shoot their way out of the subterranean locale and past all manner of rampaging zombies and resurrecting, in particular, the 'ghost' of Romero's **Day of the Dead**. This continual game of 'cat and mouse' encounters evoking the film's game origins whilst the films two most effective scenes are also responsible for eliciting some of the most pithy critical responses. Thus *The Guardian*'s Derek Malcolm was so moved by the rabid, zombie dogs Alice has to battle with, that he felt their flesh-tearing should have been expanded so that "Someone should have eaten the script and director as well." *The Observer* noted that "one unfortunate fellow is diced by a grid of laser beams, which would appear to rule out an open casket!"

The gung-ho, muscular militarism of Alice and her cohorts does have the unfortunate effect of diluting any tension as we never truly feel that she in particular, is endangered enough, a theme expanded upon in the sequel **Resident Evil:Apocalypse**, the least successful of the series both thematically and aesthetically.

Although we do learn here that the 'T-virus' had an altruistic genesis – to revive dead cells to help people regain the use of damaged limbs, this is an isolated moment of innovation as the porous plot see Major Cain (Thomas Kretschmann) ordering The Hive to be reopened – why? Inevitably, the virus escapes again and contaminates all of Racoon City or the city of the dead as it has now become. Once again ,Alice, together with mirror image – the gun-toting Jill (Sienna Guillory) and the obligatory elite forces leader Carlos (Oded Fehr), dodging zombies as they attempt to

Resident Evil:Extinction

Resident Evil:Extinction

rescue the daughter of Umbrella Corporation scientist Dr. Ashford (Jared Harris), in return for him facilitating their safe exit from the city.

The course of truly dire plots does not run smoothly however, as the final conflagration involves pitting the superhuman powers of Alice against her literal nemesis – the robotic alter ego Nemesis (Matthew G. Taylor). Alice's speed and agility versus Nemesis' slower strength could have made for an interesting encounter but director Witt shows a distinct lack of it by favouring confusing close-ups and rapidly cut action where we can see nothing of consequence, rather than a more effective combination of mid range and crane shots. Their battle, an experiment for the purposes of the Umbrella Corporation's own agenda, as explained by Major Cain; "The two of you showed such promise, but we had to see you in action. And most impressive you've been. You're like brother and sister. Heightened speed, strength, agility, the same killer instincts. Parallel strands of research. And now…we discover which is superior."

The cramped interiors and urban sprawl of the first two films are replaced with the positively agoraphobic (by comparison) Nevada desert

Resident Evil:Extinction

in **Resident Evil:Extinction**. As Jovovich explains on the ethos behind the move; "It's like a whole new world because we had the first one, which is very dark and claustrophobic. It was underground the whole time. And then in the second one you have this much bigger space, trying to escape the city. And here, it's really like the end of the world and it's all shot in daytime. It's all these very epic scenes. You've got these incredible desert sequences. It's got a completely different look, a completely different feel."

This 'different look' becomes a kind of **Night of the Living Dead** meets **Mad Max** (1979) 'car crash' in effect as Alice is rejoined by Carlos, LJ (Mike Epps), plus new survivors Claire (Ali Carter), K-Mart (Spencer Locke) and Betty (Ashanti), travelling the desert wastes in convoy to escape the zombies.

There are some incidental delights – the surreal sight of Las Vegas now all but reclaimed by the shifting desert sands, the partially buried casinos and faux Eiffel Tower emerging, barely visible (courtesy of Oscar winning Production Designer (**Pan's Labyrinth** (2006), Eugenio

Caballero), but elsewhere, the sporadic, lacklustre battles with the zombies in the sand fail to must much of a lasting impression.

Equally, the much vaunted zombie crows only serve to show how little the special effects here for such creatures have improved since the primitive titular stars in Alfred Hitchcock's **The Birds** (1963) with one characters' lame 'self sacrifice' of slamming shut the bus doors of her vehicle to contain the attacking crows and save her friends, rendered futile by the smashed windows she is surrounded by!

The only partially imaginative plot wrinkle here remains the Umbrella Corporation scientists shift in emphasis now in concentrating on trying to 'domesticate' the zombies rather than simply extirpate them (shades of **Day of the Dead** again). Their covert reasoning being to use them as 'slave labour' for the Umbrella corporation, an ironic self fulfilling prophecy when considering the real life Sony Corporations plundering of both the game and film series revenue streams to boost their own profits.

It may be a might churlish but you do have to wonder how such a global, multi-million dollar company comes to rely only on a loosely

Resident Evil:Extinction

28 Days Later

constructed chain link fence for security in the film!

A rather stronger link in the chain is provided during the opening moments however, as Alice awakes, trying to escape the Hive laboratory only to be 'killed' by one of many booby traps awaiting her and she is revealed in a neat plot conceit to be just one of many such clones who've met their deaths whilst searching for a way out – effectively Alice is killed repeatedly only to rise again in homage to the game play origins of the film series.

Ultimately, the **Resident Evil** series relies on a formulaic, evil corporate with evil scientists manipulating the masses, combated by barely dressed fugitives from zombification, utilising military weaponry together with some superhuman powers in order to survive.

There is absolutely no doubting that Jovovich can perform the physical aspects of the Alice role with some considerable élan, but as far as any emotional subtext is concerned, this characteristically remains as submerged as the Vegas landscape lying buried beneath the sand.

There may be no actual desert in Danny Boyle's **28 Days Later** but there is the explicit statement that the sands of time may have now run out for humanity. Whilst strictly speaking the 'infected' in Boyle's universe are not 'undead' and therefore not technically zombies as the director is at pains to point out, one feels that he does protest too much. So much of his iconography here betrays echoes of Romero's **The Crazies** (1973), and his (then) living dead trilogy – witness the impromptu shopping/shoplifting spree a la **Dawn of the Dead**, to the discarded newspaper buffeted open by the wind to reveal a headline of 'Evacuation" (it is 'The Dead Walk' in **Day of the Dead**), to quote but two examples.

We are firmly rooted within the realms of Darwinism from the film's opening sequence as a group of animal rights activists emancipate a number of apes from their Cambridge laboratory 'experimental prison' but only succeed in unwittingly unleashing a 'rage' virus upon the unsuspecting populace, who are all but annihilated within a month.

A bike courier who is injured and taken to hospital, awakens from a coma several days later to find the hospital deserted. As Jim (Cillian Murphy) slowly regains consciousness he begins to investigate the outside

28 Days Later

28 Weeks Later

world only to find the London streets eerily derelict as he traverses rubbish strewn streets, overturned buses and empty houses. The deafening sound of silence in what is ordinarily such a bustling cacophony of noise and vibrancy is startlingly effective. To see landmarks such as Piccadilly Circus and Westminster Bridge totally abandoned, devoid of any semblance of life is truly disquieting.

Having survived his first encounter with the 'infected' in a nearby church – no sanctuary here, merely savagery instead, Jim is 'rescued' by two street-wise survivors, Selena (Naomie Harris) and Mark (Noah Huntley). When Mark is then bitten by one of the infected Selena reacts instantly – brandishing a machete and decapitating him without hesitation. Selena's bleak 'sermon' being that "He (Mark) was full of plans. Have you got any plans Jim? Do you want us to find a cure and save the world or just fall in love and fuck? Plans are pointless. Staying alive's as good as it gets."

By hooking up with a cab driver they meet called Frank (Brendan Gleeson) and his young daughter Hannah (Megan Burns), the quartet escape the sprawling anarchy of London, encouraged by sporadic radio broadcasts optimistically advising survivors to head north to Manchester where a surviving army battalion has set up base camp. This must be the first time ever that the typically 'grim' M6 has signposted the way to 'sanctuary' rather than signposting some hellish road congestion.

Eschewing the urban confines of the capital – there's an incredibly tense (if improbable) scene where the group hurriedly change the cab's tyre in a dark tunnel, barely managing to escape from the rapidly closing infected by driving the cab 'over' a series of abandoned vehicles to the relative safety of the light outside. There is a vivid contrast with the new rural, countryside location. This verdant sense of agoraphobia is one which although effective, is rarely alluded to in the zombie genre – evoking the memory of Jorge Grau's surreal extravaganza **The Living Dead at the Manchester Morgue** (1974) where the picturesque Lake District becomes home to all manner of outlandish gore and crimson coated carnage. (Interestingly, in Fresnadillo's sequel **28 Weeks Later** there's an equally effective sequence when Donald (Robert Carlyle) flees a zombie attack on

28 Weeks Later

an isolated farmhouse, racing across the lush fields before dramatically affecting his escape in a speedboat, conveniently moored at the bank of a nearby river.

Unlike many films in this genre, Boyle also manages to convey a small fraction of the emotional angst within the decaying world, especially when related to a family environment. There is a haunting scene where Jim returns to his parents home only to discover them both lying dead together – finding a handwritten note from his mother, "With endless love, we left you sleeping. Now we're sleeping with you. Don't wake up." We identify with Jim here, our empathy begging the question of just what would you do, how would you react in such an unbearable situation?

In another sequence on their journey Jim experiences a nightmare – fearing he has been abandoned by his new friends – Frank hears him and comforts him whereupon Jim replies "Thanks Dad" in his fitful sleep, conveying the need for family, for friends and for interpersonal and social connection as a counterbalance to perhaps our more violent tendencies. Jim knows this innately but it appears to be something that Selena will have to relearn, having become desensitised by all the violence erupting around her. She does comment poignantly on Frank and Hannah's bond – "All the death. All the shit. It doesn't really mean anything to Frank and Hannah because…well, she's got a Dad and he's got his daughter. So, I was wrong when I said that staying alive is as good as it gets."

It is ironic that the rural idyll they seek under Major West's (Christopher Eccleston) leadership at the army base proves to be even more dangerous than the infected – filled streets of the capital. This is where the film transmogrifies from the realms of an effective sci-fi orientated chiller into a more visceral, action shoot-out towards the end – a dramatic change in pace and style a la **From Dusk Till Dawn** (1996). The dawning truth that it is the soldiers, mankind, as much as the infected who pose the greatest threat to civilisation is an ominous portent for the drama which unravels. As West comments; "This is what I've seen in the four weeks since infection. People killing people. Which is much what I saw in the four weeks before infection, and the four weeks before that, and before that and as far back as I care to remember. People killing people. Which to my mind, puts us in a state of normality right now."

The Darwinian themes inherent in the opening ape experiments and the dangers posed to civilisation by mankind reinforce the fact that the rage

28 Weeks Later

virus is a man made disease – we are the architects of our own doom. Given that the virus is effective within twenty seconds of transmission, according to Darwinian theory, the virus will not be an efficient survivor, the host population will soon be dead. Ditto, the virus and yet significantly, it is the probable genetic manipulation carried out in the lab which completely changes this structure.

West and his slavish troops seem to subscribe to the Herbert Spencer dictum that it will be the 'survival of the fittest' or as our friend Nietzsche would have it – back to the 'supermen' as civility is stripped away in favour of the laws of the animal kingdom to ensure survival. There's also a risible 'discussion' around the dinner table where the human race's propensity towards violence is debated but the thinly drawn West is the only soldier even partially developed so the chances for any enlightened opinions or profound comments are extremely remote.

Despite the waves of attacking rage victims outside the barracks, the most extensive threat to Selena and Hannah is the soldiers inside as they discover their intended fate, not only as the 'objects' of desire for the men, but also the means to an end, albeit this 'end' being the continuation of the species. It poses an unpalatable question as to what is the most frightening proposition – the end of the world or a surviving world populated by animalistic humans? There's a pathos inducing scene as Selena offers Hannah some valium as the soldiers wait expectantly outside the bedroom – "Are you trying to kill me" the vulnerable young girl asks with Selena's pragmatic response being "No sweetheart. I'm making you not care. Okay?"

Jim's behaviour towards the end, as he gets angrier and angrier, resorting to killing in order to ensure his own survival, leads to Selena beginning to suspect that he too has become a victim of the virus. The ambiguity is continued as a bloodied Jim tries to console a confused Selena before Hannah hits him over the head with a bottle. "Hannah, it's ok. He's not infected" Selena explains. "But I thought he was biting you" the child exclaims. "Kissing. I was kissing her. Are you stoned? A bemused and recovering Jim replies, as the close link to our innate tendency to violence is reinforced. Jim's personal journey is now complete – from his earlier

28 Weeks Later

'rebirth', awakening in hospital to the dawn of a new world, alone and vulnerable, to the conclusion where he is an embodiment of necessary violence to protect himself and his friends as well as becoming very much a realist.

His odyssey is vital to the film as Boyle prefers to concentrate on the human survival instinct as opposed to the how's and why's of the virus outbreak, which owes its identity to the numerous diseases to have plagued the world over the last decade and beyond – be they AIDS, SARS, Foot and mouth, MRSA or Blue tongue.

At one point Jim questions rather naively; "What do you mean there's no government? There's always a government, they're in a bunker or plane somewhere!" This distinct lack of authority present throughout the film aids the vacuum for uncontrolled violence which occurs in its wake with the resulting anarchy causing the characters to speculate regarding the kind of world they will be (hopefully) living in. Any such existential thoughts, as Selena ponders with Jim – "You were thinking that you'll never hear another piece of original music ever again. You'll never read a book that hasn't already been written or see a film that hasn't already been shot" are jettisoned due to the frantic pace during the second half of the film. This also deprives us of any opportunity to fully explore the military/civilian divide with so many characters to concentrate on (or not, as the case may be). It's also worth noting that Boyle and scriptwriter Alex Garland originally intended to focus on the original four protagonists but this would have left too close a similarity to Romero's **Dawn of the Dead**.

Boyle's somewhat controversial use of digital cameras gives the film a punchy immediacy as well as a rather grainy, ugly hue in parts – with a dystopian grime permeating the closing scenes played out almost entirely against a (typically?!) Mancunian backdrop of incessant rain. In contrast, the upbeat coda which sees Jim, Selena and Hannah welcoming a plane flying overhead to their new coastal retreat, is shot on film as if to reinforce the euphoric effect.

With Boyle handing over the directorial reins to Fresnadillo for the sequel **28 Weeks Later** – London, or more specifically the Isle of Dogs is now a US army controlled quarantine zone, a kind of Ballardian refuge colony if you will.

There is a bravura opening sequence set in a remote farmhouse which undergoes a frenzied attack from the infected. The haunting image where the aforementioned Dan manages to flee, but only by leaving behind his wife Alice (Catherine McCormack) to a bloody 'demise' is undoubtedly the film's highpoint.

The remainder defies credibility as Dan's two children manage to escape the heavily guarded Wharf area, find their mother still alive in the family home but now infected, before Don's 'lowly' caretaker character gains access to the lab where his wife is now being held, by using only a swipe card?! After an impromptu exchange of all manner of bodily fluids, Don now joins the ranks of the infected, continuing to pop up like a pantomime villain when you least expect him.

With trite dialogue, proliferated with 'code reds' and 'green zones' the height of military intellect leaves the considered opinion to be to call in an air strike and raise the entire area to the ground – infected and innocent victims alike. The one shred of interest here is the notion that Don's children may indeed contain a 'cure' for the rage virus within their genetic make up so their safety becomes paramount amidst the numerous chase sequences and graphic carnage which ensues.

The tension and intrigue of Boyle's opus are all but forgotten save for some effective moments with the survivors escaping the infected and a good use of several London locations including the new Wembley Stadium for the finale. When put in a wider context though, the three 'R's – Repression, Rage and Resurrection of the zombie genre looks set to keep on reviving and reinventing itself for some time to come. The living are dead. Long live the undead!

BENEATH DARK WATERS

Jim Harper

The global success of **Ring** (1998) turned Hideo Nakata into one of Japan's most important directors and an internationally sought-after figure. Aside from the respectable (if flawed) **Ring 2** (1999), it would be another four years before Nakata's subtle, chilling ghosts were let out of the closet. After branching out with the teen romance of **The Sleeping Bride** (2000) and the complex kidnap thriller **Chaos** (2000), Nakata returned to the genre that had made him famous with 2002's **Dark Water** (Honogurai Mizu no Soko kara), arguably his second best film. In practical terms, **Dark Water** has much in common with **Ring**: it's also based on a Kôji Suzuki story and produced by Takashige Ichise, while both films feature the same cinematographer (Junichirô Hayashi) and editor (Nobuyuki Takahashi). However, **Dark Water** is not simply a recycled version of its predecessor. Although both are ghost stories with a strong western influence, **Dark Water** is a character-driven piece that drops the 'high-concept' components (the curse, the urban legends and the technophobic paranoia) in favour of dramatic and emotional elements. Although ultimately it is a less successful film than **Ring**, in many respects these changes make it a more interesting and mature piece of work.

The central figure is Yoshimi Matsubara (Hitomi Kuroki), a single mother trying to find a new home for her and her five-year-old daughter Ikuko (Rio Kanno), while fighting an acrimonious custody battle with her unpleasant ex-husband. More out of desperation than desire, she moves into a gloomy-looking old-fashioned apartment building. The apartment itself is damp and miserable, but Yoshimi needs to show the courts that she can provide Ikuko with a stable home, so they move in. Despite their problems, things are going fairly well for the family: Ikuko is attending a good kindergarten, and Yoshimi finds herself a job working as a proof-reader at a local publisher.

It's not long before the cracks begin to show, however. The patch of damp on the ceiling has developed a steady drip, and neither the aged building manager (Isao Yuda, from **Ring 2** and **Juon: The Grudge**) or the letting agent are particularly interested in doing anything about it. It's an old

Dark Water

building, they say, and old buildings sometimes leak. Poor plumbing is not the only problem. The water might be coming from the apartment upstairs, but no one is ever home. No one's home, but the sound of footsteps- a child's footsteps- can clearly be heard coming through the ceiling below. There are no other children living in the building, but there's a child's bag on the roof; Ikuko wants to keep it, but her hygiene-conscious mother throws it away. A few days later, it's back on the roof. And if there are no other children in the building, then who is the short, yellow-coated figure that Yoshimi has seen, once again on the roof?

Yoshimi is not the only one who has seen the figure; her daughter has seen her several times, often at the kindergarten. After the second of these incidents, Ikuko faints, and Yoshimi is called to the school. In conversation with the principle, she discovers who the yellow-coated figure is: Mitsuko Kawai, a local girl who disappeared on her way home from the kindergarten two years earlier. Her home, as Yoshimi soon realises, was the apartment above theirs, where all the water is coming from, Growing ever more frantic, Yoshimi begins to pack once again, convinced that Mitsuko has returned to the building and intends to take Ikuko away. Worried that her increasingly irrational behaviour is threatening her chances of retaining custody, Yoshimi's sympathetic solicitor manages to convince her that there is a rational explanation for these events; if the apartment above hers has been unlocked since Mitsuko's father left over a year ago, anybody could have gained entry, with the taps left running until they flooded the apartment and soaked through to the rooms below. Reassured, Yoshimi resolves to keep her emotions and her imagination in check, and to focus on fighting the custody battle. For a moment it looks as if everything might be okay after all; but then the bag appears again, this time in their apartment. As the tensions reach breaking point, Yoshimi is forced to confront Mitsuko and uncover the truth about her death and her designs on Ikuko.

While the basic plot- family moves into a new home that also has a few supernatural residents- has been a staple of the horror genre for many years, **Dark Water** belongs to a more select group that is epitomized by Jack Clayton's Henry James adaptation **The Innocents** (1961), Robert Wise's 1963 classic **The Haunting**, and most recently, Alejandro Amenábar's **The Others** (2001). All of these films are built around unstable female characters whose supernatural experiences may or may not be a product of their own fragile psychological state. Often these characters are single mothers- or mother-figures, as in **The Innocents**- struggling to cope with the pressures of life and motherhood with little or no support from anyone else. In interviews Nakata has acknowledged the influence of **The Innocents** and **The Haunting** upon his work, including one scene in **Dark Water**- in which Yoshimi sees her daughter running out of the elevator and wonders exactly whose hand she is holding- that is highly reminiscent of the latter film. In keeping with the director's love of British cinema, there are also nods to **Don't Look Now** (1973)- the small, rain-coated figure, often glimpsed but rarely fully visible- and Stanley Kubrick's **The Shining** (1980), with the deluge of water that appears when the elevator doors open. It's also tempting to draw parallels between **Dark Water** and Roman Polanski's **Repulsion** (1965), as the physical decay of Yoshimi's apartment- specifically, the ever-spreading patch of damp and mold- comes to symbolise her own mental decline. However, Nakata is smart enough to pay tribute to his favourite films without appropriating them wholesale, and the credit for **Dark Water**'s most effective moments is rightfully his.

Even so, it's interesting to note that little of the story had to be altered in order to prepare it for western audiences, with Walter Salles' 2004 remake remaining largely faithful to the Japanese original.

Dark Water represents Nakata's most in-depth examination of one of his most prominent themes, the breakdown of the family unit. Although it was only part of the background in 1996's **Ghost Actress** (as seen in the film that Murai is directing), the theme achieved a greater significance in **Ring**. Both **Ring** and **Dark Water** focus on single mothers, while dysfunctional family relations are the catalyst for the supernatural chain of events: Sadako's mother abandoned her by committing suicide, leaving her to be slain by her father, while the failure of Mitsuko's parents to properly take care of their child leads to her tragic accidental death. This is not only the case with Nakata's horror films: infidelity lies at the heart of the web of murder and deceit that runs through **Chaos**, while even the handyman's background features yet another broken marriage. Much of **Dark Water**'s emotional resonance comes from the similarity between Yoshimi's childhood and Mitsuko's, since both were raised by mothers who had little time for them and eventually abandoned them altogether. The pattern is repeating itself with Ikuko and her father: he is only interested in using the child as a means to attack his ex-wife, caring little about her personal welfare. But these things are never black and white; ironically, by the end of **Dark Water** Yoshimi is forced to accept that the best thing she can do for Ikuko is to leave her with her father and become Mitsuko's surrogate mother.

To his credit, for the most part Nakata manages to strike a careful balance between the drama and the horror, making sure that one does not overpower the other. Although the film's climax- when Yoshimi tells Ikuko to stay away from her- is undeniably melodramatic, it's preceded by the genuinely horrific sight of the decomposed, water-bloated Mitsuko throwing herself at Yoshimi with an ear-piercing shriek. Once again Nakata's efforts are supported by a memorable score from Kenji Kawai, who also scored **The Sleeping Bride** and **Chaos**, as well as Mamoru Oshii's **Avalon** (2001) and both **Ghost in the Shell** films. His work on **Dark Water** is less alien and discordant than **Ring**'s heavily processed metallic noise, but it's also entirely appropriate, often evoking the muted clanging of water pipes. Less memorable are the melodic strings that Kawai adds to the film's more melodramatic moments, however. **Dark Water**'s main flaw is the unnecessary epilogue, where the now-teenaged Ikuko (played by Asami Mizukawa, later in 2004's **Shibuya Kaidan**) returns to their apartment to find her mother still there, still caring for Mitsuko. It adds little to the story except another dose of sentimentality. Although on the whole the original is the superior work, the American version found a more satisfactory way of ending the film, with the daughter meeting her mother in the elevator for a final, brief farewell.

Along with **Ghost Actress**, **Ring** and **Chaos**, **Dark Water** was optioned for an American remake. The film eventually appeared in 2004, directed by Brazillian Walter Salles and starring Jennifer Connelly, Pete Postlethwaite and Tim Roth. Although the location was shifted to New York, the American **Dark Water** is almost entirely faithful to the events of Nakata's version. However, Salles does remove or reduce the 'horror' elements of the story, instead choosing to focus on the human drama. Ironically enough- given Nakata's personal preference for melodrama- the remake is more melodramatic that the original. By lessening the role of the supernatural, more support is given to the possibility that the events

Dark Water

are a product of Connelly's anxiety and instability, while the suggestion that she is slowly becoming more and more like her own dysfunctional mother is made explicit. More significant is Connelly's realisation that she needs her ex-husband's help to raise the child. In Nakata's film, Yoshimi understands that the only way to save her daughter's life is to leave the child with her father; even before the climax Connelly comes to realise that she isn't up to the task of raising her daughter alone. Yoshimi's ex-husband is a vindictive troublemaker, but the in US version (as played by Dougray Scott) Salles establishes his genuine concern for the child's welfare.

Curiously enough, much of **Dark Water**'s plot appeared in Nakata's US debut, the Ehren Kruger-scripted **The Ring Two**, which appeared only a few weeks before Salles' version of the film. This time Samara's motives are exactly the same as Mitsuko's, making **The Ring Two** a curious hybrid of **Dark Water** and Gore Verbinski's **The Ring**. Despite Nakata's best efforts, he is unable to overcome the flaws of Kruger's script, and **The Ring Two** stands as perhaps his weakest film overall.

In contrast, the original **Dark Water** is one of the director's finest works, and his second bona fide classic of modern Japanese horror. Although not as influential as **Ring**, **Dark Water** did provide one new archetype for Japanese filmmakers to recycle: the image of a young girl as 'vengeful spirit'. Before 2002, the majority of ghosts were adult females- like **Ring**'s Sadako and Kayako from the **Juon** series- but Mitsuko Kawai quickly became the template for a number of other phantoms, in films such as **Juon: The Grudge 2** (2003), **The Locker** (**Shibuya Kaidan**, 2004) and **Pray** (2005).

(This article is an extract from the forthcoming book by Jim Harper from Noir Publishing - *Flowers From Hell - The Modern Japanese Horror Film*)

RURAL GOTHIC

Andy Black

"I am the devil and I am here to do the devil's work." Otis B. Driftwood (Bill Moseley) in Rob Zombie's **The Devil's Rejects** (2005).

"Happiness lies in the senses and virtue gratifies none of them." The Marquis De Sade

When Rob Zombie's first directorial outing **House of a 1000 Corpses** (2003) was dropped by craven Universal executives for being an 'uber celebration of depravity', their intended insult of Zombie's opus only served in making it become a kind of 'cause celebre' or 'holy grail' for the horror cognoscenti, who no doubt rejoiced *en masse* when the film was rescued from celluloid limbo by Lions Gate for release some three years late.

Zombie's fan boy love of Wes Craven's **The Last House on the Left** (1972) and especially Tobe Hooper's **The Texas Chain Saw Massacre** (1974) greatly informs his debut feature. When two young college couples Jerry Goldsmith (sic) (Chris Hardwick), Denise (Erin Daniels), Mary (Jennifer Jostyn) and Bill (Rainn Wilson) embark on a cross country trip through the American backwaters, they discover the legend of Dr. Satan – an infamous medic who took to mutilating his mental patients before being dispatched himself from the 'Hanging Tree'. As the quartet search in vain for this grotesque landmark, all they succeed in uncovering is a hitchhiker, Baby (Sheri Moon) who leads them to an isolated farmhouse inhabited by a cannibalistic family with a penchant for satanic rituals – cue the introduction to the nefarious Otis Driftwood (Bill Moseley) and Mother Firefly (Karen Black).

Sounds familiar? Yep, this is an avowedly Hooper-esque 'set-up' and, as such, the shadow of **The Texas Chain Saw Massacre** series envelops the entire film – even down to actor Moseley 'reprising' his equally repulsive turn as Chop Top in **The Texas Chain Saw Massacre 2** (1986).

We become embroiled in the rural/urban, redneck/white trash

Monster Man

divide which epitomises not just **House of a 1000 Corpses** but a plethora of similarly themed entries including Wes Craven's **The Hills Have Eyes** (1977) and **The Hills Have Eyes 2** (1985), Alexandre Aja's remake **The Hills Have Eyes** (2006), Martin Weisz's **The Hills Have Eyes 2** (2007), Eli Roth's **Cabin Fever** (2002), Marcus Nispel's 'reimagining' **The Texas Chain Saw Massacre** (2003), Michael Davis' **Monster Man** (2003) and Alexandre Aja's **Switchblade Romance** (2003).

A stark contrast is presented between the close, insular (frequently inbred) communities of rural America, cultural and economic backwaters where any new visitors from out of town are instantly condemned to social pariah status by virtue of their differing background and attitudes.

In Davis' **Monster Man**, Adam (Eric Jungmann) is the nice guy, reluctant 'hero' with the loud mouthed and uncouth 'friend' Harley (Justin Urich), travelling into redneck country and upsetting the locals. As Harley sits in a bar observing the clientele soaking up a monster truck competition on TV, he crassly announces that; "These fucking rednecks must have IQ's the same size as my underwear to watch this!" It's the metallic monster truck outside however, that they need to worry about, complete with snapping jaws ready to run them of the road like a mechanical crocodile toying with its prey.

Part road movie – "on this highway the road kill is human" with its echoes of Steven Spielberg's **Duel** (1971) and part monster mayhem as the nubile hitchhiker Sarah (Aimee Brooks) succeeds only in leading the duo to the isolated lair where they are required as unwilling organ donors for the grotesque (and atrophying) Brother Fred (Joe Goodrich).

Given all the 'toilet' humour that Harvey indulges in, appropriately the most effective sequence finds Adam locking himself into a cubicle as the repugnant 'monster man' of the title enters the washroom – all peeling walls and fetid atmosphere, whilst outside the slovenly Harley stands astride the truck's cab happily urinating onto the seat inside!

Coincidentally, a similarly tense gas station scene is also played out in Aja's **Switchblade Romance**, only this time the hulking killer is Le Teuer (Philippe Nahon). Having previously burst into an isolated farmhouse before killing Alexia's (Maiwenn Le Besco) parents and kidnapping the

Switchblade Romance

startled girl in his van, the killer remains unaware of the presence of her close friend Marie (Cecile De France), who is secretly pursuing them.

By utilising the special effects maestro Gianetti De Rossi of Lucio Fulci's **Zombie** (1979) and **House by the Cemetery** (1981) fame, Aja instantly betrays his 'video nasties' influences, deliberately upping the gore quotient to appease the horror crowd. A heady mix of unrequited lesbianism (in Marie's covert feelings for Alexia), an unremitting visceral charge as blood spills, flows and sprays from every orifice and a bravura coda offering a gruesome play on the split personality genre, creates a highly ambitious if emotionally detaching finale.

"To dull to be a desecration" was one of the 'kinder' comments ushering in Marcus Nispel's controversial **The Texas Chain Saw Massacre** remake – perhaps there are some much vaunted classics which are held in such revere that the remake button should never ever be pushed – think **Psycho** (1960) and (1998), together with **The Wicker Man** (1973) and (2006) for instance.

It may have the gore, it may have some style, it may even have the statuesque Jessica Biel as Erin, running around in the rain and sweating profusely in a tight fitting t-shirt, but no 'family dinner' scene? It's like Psycho without the shower murder. Only R. Lee Ermey as Sheriff Hoyt seems to be enjoying himself, but the rural isolation and inherent suspense this causes in Hooper's original is sorely missed here, as to are the more outlandish family of 'freaks' and cannibals. Even Leatherface (Andrew Bryniarski) himself is given an appallingly 'politically correct' make over as we learn he was bullied as a child at school because of his disfigured face – the basis for his homicidal tendencies now!

No such liberal displays in Eli Roth's **Cabin Fever**, except perhaps in the copious amounts of blood expended as five college friends embark on a vacation in a rural (and decidedly redneck) retreat - a log cabin nestling in some remote woods. Having briefly met the decidedly unfriendly locals they also encounter a lone hermit who unfortunately happens to be incubating a virulent flesh eating virus (based on the real life nacrotising fasciitis) but playing rather more as an AIDS panic here, and the virus is spread amongst the group.

With a corpse lying in the nearby reservoir to spread the contagion to the local populace in the water supply and enough group infighting to result in the infected Karen (Jordan Ladd) being shut outside in the shed

and effectively left to die, Roth highlights both the rising tensions between the protagonists and the different ways they react to the extreme situation, together with the ever present antipathy between the 'outsiders' invading this rural retreat and thus shattering the status quo enjoyed by the locals.

By treating both sex and the body as areas of revulsion, a personal battleground if you will, Roth is treading similar territory to the master of 'body horror', David Cronenberg and recalling some of his earlier work such as **Shivers** (1975) and **Rabid** (1977), with an especially gruelling sequence where leg shaving becomes just that.

With the obligatory sequel now in the works entitled **Cabin Fever 2:Spring Fever** scheduled for 2008 release and under the tutelage of Ti West, the contemporaneous theme here is for the attendees to a high school prom becoming contaminated by drinking a well known brand of bottled water…

Zombie effectively eschews this trendy posturing and fashionable philosophising by grounding his characters with both a Sadean zeal for inflicting violence and torture whilst also exhibiting a cartoonish buffoonery at times, evoking both the thrill of a fairground ride and the cheesy horrors of the funhouse.

Sid Haig's audacious turn as the clowning Captain Spaulding is both pantomime villain and a grotesque parody of human nature rolled into one wicked persona. "Ya'll think us folk from the country's real funny-like, dontcha?" he chides the college students in **House of a 1000 Corpses**. With his Museum of Monsters and Madmen doubling up as a convenience store and fried chicken joint (!), he's an eccentric character – even when shooting a would be shoplifter he complains the "Goddamn, motherfucker got blood all over my best clown suit." His later exchange with Stucky (Michael J. Pollard) about one miscreant concerns sticking *Planet of the Apes* dolls up his "asshole" – "They had to take him to the hospital. The kid had Dr. Zaius stuck halfway up his butt and they couldn't get it out!"

This surreal humour continues unabated, heightened if anything in Zombie's assured follow up **The Devil's Rejects**. There's a jaw-dropping sequence where Spaulding ushers a bewildered kid and his mum from out of their car so he can escape in it. "I'm gonna have to be taking your car today. See I have some top secret clown business that supersedes any plans that you might have for this here vehicle" Spaulding solemnly explains. "What's that about clown business?" is the mother's reply. "Do I stutter, bitch?" comes the bombastic response.

When the 'good' Captain's appearance has the boy crying, he questions; "What's the matter kid? Don't ya like clowns?…Why? Don't we make ya laugh? Aren't we fuckin' funny? You best come up with an answer, cos' I'm gonna come back here and check on you and your momma and if you ain't got a reason why you hate clowns I'm gonna kill your whole fucking family." Cue more child crying – "All right, now get your fuckin' ass out of the car, go on yayayaya" Spaulding orders whilst simultaneously laughing.

There's also an incredible exchange when Sheriff Wydell (William Forsythe) is trailing the dysfunctional Firefly family – named after Marx Brothers characters, and resorts to bringing in a film critic Marty (Robert Trebor) to help trace them. His reaction – to bring in Groucho for questioning! When Marty has the temerity to inform him that he died in 1977, three days after "that goddamn fucking Elvis Presley", the 'king' loving Sheriff goes ballistic – "Son, if you ever say another derogatory word about Elvis Aaron Presley in my presence again, I will kick the living

House of a 1000 Corpses

House of a 1000 Corpses

shit out of you."

In addition to this extreme humour Zombie also ups the ante with a bravura road kill sequence where the shell shocked Wendy (Kate Norby) – having survived the physical and mental torture meted out by Otis and Baby, then proceeds to run out onto the desert road for help, only to be summarily trampled over by a large oncoming truck – as a choked Sheriff Dwyer exclaims; "Jesus Christ, what a fucking mess. There must be a hundred yards of bloody asphalt and corpse chunks", as he surveys the 'body' now flattened over the road cartoon style.

This bleak, avowedly outlandish humour is used to counteract the flagrant brutality and wanton violence of the family and Otis in particular, whilst Baby's ingénue is only a fledgling crazy with her collection of dismembered dolls. In **House of a 1000 Corpses** she revels in tormenting the college kids now imprisoned in the Firefly house – "Take his gag out. It's more fun with the screaming" she yells excitedly as the usually composed (!) Jerry (Goldsmith) pleads for his life. When she and Otis are holed up in a roadside motel in **The Devil's Rejects** she gets equal kicks from

House of a 1000 Corpses

toying with their unfortunate captives – enticing Roy (Geoffrey Lewis) as he mischievously asks her "Do you kiss your mama with that mouth?" – "Trust me, fella. That ain't the only thing I do with this mouth."

House of a 1000 Corpses remains Zombie's learning curve, experimenting with split screens, random inserts of grainy 'snuff' styled footage and psychedelic colours – rejoicing in its' 'B-movie' origins, the ultimate cheesy horror film pastiche with acerbic dialogue and wit. And clearly, just as say Romero sympathises with his zombies as opposed to the human characters, so too does Zombie revel in the guilty pleasures to be had with Otis and co. The 'good guys' are just too bland and vapid to arouse our interest and therefore our empathy. The eclectic motifs ranging from serial killers to crazy families with clowns, satanic worshippers and eccentric doctors thrown into this hallucinating mix of a film.

Although some scenes are just too busy, betraying Zombie's music video origins, the final third of the film undergoes a change in emphasis as we discover the outré underworld of the hideous Dr. Satan – a labyrinth of dark tunnels hiding even darker secrets and horrors – very reminiscent of

the subterranean lair in **The Texas Chain Saw Massacre 2**.

There's an almost sinister, poetic feel to the scenes such as when the Sheriff's deputies check this queasy hell hole of a house with Slim Whitman's "I Remember You" accompanying the violence as if in a surreal homage to Stanley Kubrick's **A Clockwork Orange** (1971). Likewise, there's a lugubrious fatalism to the image of a coffin being slowly lowered into the murky waters below during the film's climax.

If **House of a 1000 Corpses** is Zombie's training ground then **The Devil's Rejects** is most definitely the real thing – a veritable tour de force as the director paints with a much wider, more confident brush, beginning to create his own mythos rather than raiding other peoples as the villainous characters emerge to even greater effect in contrast to the insipid (by comparison) victims.

To this end, Otis, who cuts a Charles Manson-esque figure, expands his 'philosophy' to a victim in **House of a 1000 Corpses** thus, "Listen, you Malibu middle class Barbie piece of shit. I'm trying to work here. Work? You ever work? Yeah, I'll bet you have. Scoopin' ice cream to your shit-

The Devil's Rejects

The Devil's Rejects

heel friends on summer break. Well I ain't talkin' about no goddamn white socks with Mickey Mouse on one side and Donald Duck on the other. I ain't readin' no funny books, mama. Our bodies come and go but this blood… is forever."

His later rant to a room of tied up cheerleaders (!), continues his wholly unique brand of ranting – "Why" you ask? "Why" is not the question. How. Now that is a question worth examining. How could I, being born of such, uh…conventional stock, arrive a leader of the rebellion? An escapist from a conformist world, destined to find happiness only in that which cannot be explained? I brought you here for a reason, but unfortunately you and your sentimental minds are doing me no good! My brain is frozen. Locked! I have to break free from this culture of mechanical reproductions and the thick encrustations dying on the surface." When he sees the girls are not understanding, "Oh Christ. Fuck it!" is the considered wisdom he vents forth.

From the soaring crane shot of the Firefly ranch with a pigs head skewered defiantly on the metal framework above, zombie is signalling

House of a 1000 Corpses

his intent, dispensing with the former films claustrophobia in favour of a patently more agoraphobic approach in **The Devil's Rejects,** with vast expanses of road filling the frame and open spaces bleached by the burning sun. With freeze frames, southern rock drawl in place of formulaic heavy metal and a plethora of Sergio Leone-styled, tight close-ups of sweaty faces, Zombie may still be "genuflecting at the altar of Hooper and Peckinpah" but he adds his own idiosyncratic approach and now customary droll language to propel the story at an even pace.

Zombie's encyclopaedic familiarity with the horror genre – populating the film with his own cult figures in Ken Foree (**Dawn of the Dead**), Michael Berryman (**The Hills Have Eyes**), P. J. Soles (**Halloween**) and Mary Woronov (**Eating Raoul**), plus Moseley's Otis reprising a repulsive face swap routine from **The Texas Chain Saw Massacre 2**, ensures his popularity with horror fans.

The continual blurring in the boundaries between sex and violence – be it Sheriff Wydell's 'phallic' stabbing of Mother Firefly (Leslie Easterbrook) as she 'flirts' with him in prison, positively encouraging any advances or in the prolonged torture of the musicians in the motel (shades of **From Dusk Till Dawn** here) – "I think I can still smell your wife's pussy on my gun…hope it doesn't rust the barrel" Otis taunts at one point, also recalls the 'grindhouse' films of the seventies with their ambiguous morality and levels of villainy, there are no heroes, just seemingly hapless victims and characters whose interest factor rises in direct correlation to their levels of depravity. Take Otis' not too veiled warning to one victim, "Boy, the next word that comes out of your mouth better be some brilliant fuckin' Mark Twain shit. 'Cause it's definitely getting chiselled on your tombstone." He is safe in the knowledge that no such profundity will ever be forthcoming.

If divine intervention is the only chance of salvation for the victims then this feeds Otis the perfect opportunity to mock the seemingly absent Lord – "I want you to pray to your God. I want you to pray that he comes and saves you. I want lightning to come and crash down upon my fucking head" he rants.

In the distinct absence of any real spiritual guidance or presence,

House of a 1000 Corpses

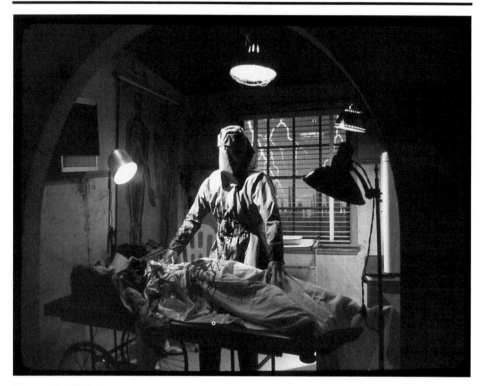

House of a 1000 Corpses

he mocks again – "Ooh aahh. I feel it! Oh great god almighty I repent, I repent! Oh I feel the love of god, god. God almighty! Oh the Holy Spirit is in my body."

As if this moral anarchy wasn't enough to bear, Zombie increases the mayhem as we see the transformation in Otis' nemesis, Sheriff Wydell, whose increasingly brutal and brazen disregard for human life sees him becoming as sadistic as his 'prey' even to the point where having overpowered the family, it is he who becomes the torturer and the family the victims. Bizarrely our sympathies shift as we almost begin to empathise with the murderous clan rather than the forces of law and order.

This seismic shift is one of the most inveigling aspects of the film – early in the action the Sheriff outlines his 'manifesto' to his deputy, "Dying is not an option. Now stick that back in that grey matter of yours and you make that stick. 'Cause any other thought is gonna get you cold slab, toe tag and mailed home to your mamma in a plastic bag. Are we crystal?"

As Zombie himself has attempted to vindicate his confrontational approach by maintaining that "this movie does not glorify violence, it shows how ugly and nasty it is."

Wydell gradually but surely embodies this 'nastiness' – "I'm going to kill every member of your family. They're going to feel the pain and suffering of every last victim!" This is delivered as a promise rather than a threat as Wydell later dispatches Mother Firefly to begin the cycle of retribution. The Sheriff's rapidly disintegrating rationale is glimpsed as his quasi-evangelical eulogy is delivered thus' "From delusion lead me to truth, from darkness lead me to light, from death lead me to eternal life. Hallelujah! Are you feeling it brother?!

Near the climax of the film as Wydell lords it over the now captive family, tied to chairs in the flame-filled basement of their ranch, the Sheriff sounds off – "You know I got to thank you all…for helping me understand what my heritage is. You see the Wydell's, they've always been vigilante justice. Now my grand-daddy, he rode with the likes of Tom Horn killin' scum like you for a livin'. We've always been devil slayers."

He continues with some zeal – "Wake up! See, I tried to walk the line but now I realise there is no line. Now we here, we are playin' on a level that most will never see. I know my brother George, he didn't see it." Spaulding (chiding him on the fact that the family had killed him previously) quips, "Maybe he had a divine moment when his brains hit the floor." "Yeah well, maybe you will too" counters the Sheriff.

In escaping this conflagration and meeting a police roadblock with the subsequent hail of bullets as they drive on unnervingly in their car, Otis, Baby and Spaulding play out to the evocative strains on the soundtrack of Lynyrd Skynyrd's epic *Free Bird* – an appropriate title for these 'free spirits' to bow out on.

The great challenge for Zombie will be to see if he can now build upon this ingenuity by thinking 'outside the box' and away from his cult film comfort zone to develop further his undoubted talent. The fact that he chose to remake **Halloween** (2007) this year suggests perhaps he is not quite ready yet – it will certainly be a great pity if he cannot make, or at least attempt, the leap sometime in the future.

INDEX OF FILMS
Page Number in bold indicates an illustration